Begin with "I"

An inspiring journey to transform You into You+

notionpress
.com

Begin with "I"

An inspiring journey to transform You into You+

Rohit Sethi

notionpress.com

Notion Press

Old No. 38, New No. 6

McNichols Road, Chetpet

Chennai - 600 031

First Published by Notion Press 2015

ISBN: 978-93-52060-80-1

Mom and dad,

you know what this means to me.

It would never have been possible without you,

I dedicate this book to you!

ACKNOWLEDGEMENT

I have read hundreds of books to date and I always read the acknowledgements section carefully to really understand what made the book come alive into this world. For years, I have been wishing to share my ideas and I knew I would write a book 'someday' (yes, that's the typical timeframe by when most of us want to achieve our dreams!). Now since that 'someday' has come, let me express my sincere gratitude to all those who helped making it possible.

I consider myself blessed to have some amazingly wonderful people around me in the form of close friends, family members and acquaintances, who played their own special roles in making this book go from a wish to a finished product in your hands.

If I really have to name a few (and please forgive me if I miss including you below, I still remain grateful to you and it would not make your contribution to this book any lesser), I would like to thank:

- Sangeeta Sethi Kakkar: You personify love, excellence and leadership; you are the best sister!
- Tushar Prakash, Samrat Bose, IshwinderJeet Singh, Nitin Veeresh, Petra Chidiac and Suhyeon Park: Thank you for bearing with me all this time; you are people of great strength, insight and patience!
- Krishnan Vaidyanathan, Keshav Chugh and Bala Kumaran: Thank you for pushing me over the edge; you guys manifest possibilities!

And last but not the least, a big thank you to NotionPress for leading this very important project for me!

CONTENTS

INTRODUCTION

Dear Reader,

Many thanks for reaching out and choosing to invest your valuable time in this book.

With this book, I would like to invite you to a journey into our inner worlds where we together understand how through undertaking of this journey, we can seamlessly take our lives to the next level no matter where we are currently.

In the following pages, you will not only receive the findings from my own experience, but also those that I have summarized from hundreds of books, tapes, seminars and interviews that I have accumulated over the past sixteen years of my life, as I continue this exciting quest for understanding the fundamental variables that define the quality of peoples' lives. Feel free to view me as a mere conduit, passing down wisdom of the ages from numerous enlightened souls and view this book as a reminder, of those simple, universal and obvious sounding rules that help make life more 'fulfilling' and 'enriched'.

We all lead busy day-to-day lives. I myself keep quite busy with the demands of making a living and so I fully understand that our lives are ruled by defined patterns that we run day-in and day-out to make everything function smoothly. We resist major changes to these familiar patterns. **My key intent through this book is to introduce you to those core principles and exercises that can have maximum impact on your life without you really needing to spend your limited time reading about and practicing hundreds of tools and techniques published around these areas.** In addition, I want to demonstrate how easily we can integrate these principles and exercises into our busy lives, as there is no rush to apply all of them at the same time, become overwhelmed with the much disruption they cause and then stop. A better strategy is to learn one skill at a time, practise it till it becomes natural and then move onto the next one.

Two more ideas that you will be able to appreciate through this book are: (i) the ability to step out and look at ourselves both, in the present and in the future, is a key enabler in our personal development, and (ii) the people we surround ourselves with, play a critical role in determining the quality of our lives, and we can actually use their power on us to help achieve our goals.

If you are new to self-help and personal development, I can assure you that this book will provide you with most of what you need to become your best self and continue pushing further. If you get more interested in any particular area, feel free to follow more established experts to further enhance your understanding in that area. If you are already a self-help enthusiast, this book will serve as a quick reminder of the key principles and high-impact exercises.

If you find the style of writing a bit conversational and unconventional, please be aware that it is intentional. This is the age of distraction where getting peoples' time and attention is tougher than it has ever been in the past. Also, to be honest, more than demonstrating my literary prowess (there are many established authors you can read for that!), my intent is to ensure that the readers get my message in the simplest and quickest manner.

Every effort has been made to give credit where it is due for the material contained herein. As I constantly read, watch videos, attend seminars, and collect ideas, I may have inadvertently referenced your work without attribution. If I have done so, please accept my apologies and let me know so I can credit you in the next edition.

Thanks again for giving me a chance to talk to you. I appreciate your choice and it is with great respect that I begin this relationship with you as together we begin this journey into individuality, inspiration and intensity to realize our highest potentials *(these concepts have been detailed in the book).*

I truly wish that you like what you read and these words make a positive difference to your life.

Happy transforming! Let's begin with 'I'!

Love,
Rohit

"Our deepest fear is not that we are inadequate.

Our deepest fear is that we are powerful beyond measure.

It is our light, not our darkness that most frightens us.

We ask ourselves, Who am I to be brilliant, gorgeous, talented, fabulous?

Actually, who are you not to be?

You are a child of God.

Your playing small does not serve the world."

~Marianne Williamson, requoted by Nelson Mandela

1. RON, THE AVERAGE GUY!

This is a short story about a guy called Ron. Ron is 30 years old and has done a fairly good job at convincing himself all these years, especially the last few years that he has spent working in a corporate job, that he is an 'average' guy. Now, since Ron himself is so convinced of it, I don't think the world can do much about it, so let me start by introducing Ron as a 30-year-old average guy.

Ron is an average guy, not so much because of anything else, as much as he himself being convinced of it!

Like most of us, Ron went to college so he could make a decent living. He wakes up in the morning, gets ready and joins two of his colleagues living close by, in a car pool to reach office. Ron lives the typical week-in week-out life of a professional, eagerly waiting for weekends, most of which are spent catching up on rest and hanging out with friends. The latter is more applicable in the case of single people, and since Ron is single, this is how he ends up spending most of his time.

It has been six years since Ron has completed his MBA. He loves to spend time on social networks like most people of this generation. However, sometimes his mind gets totally hijacked. He feels like he is doing 'not-so-well' in his own life when he sees what his batchmates have been up to all these years. Some seem to have progressed really fast in their jobs and are handling fairly senior roles. A couple of them who started their own companies are now featuring on national television and raising millions of dollars in foreign investment. Some others, who were clear on their priority to build a family, got married early and now look quite happy with their kids growing up fast and strong. Some others seem to have begun devoting time to more standard activities such as running, blogging, painting, cooking, photography, dancing, and traveling to get their creative releases that the typical corporate jobs do not fully allow. Oh yes, add bungee jumping and skydiving to the list as well!

Absorbing all this information from the social networks, Ron's mind tends to quickly construct a guy who has done all of these things – someone who is progressing fast in his career, runs marathons, vacations abroad, invests his money wisely in building assets and has a happy family life.

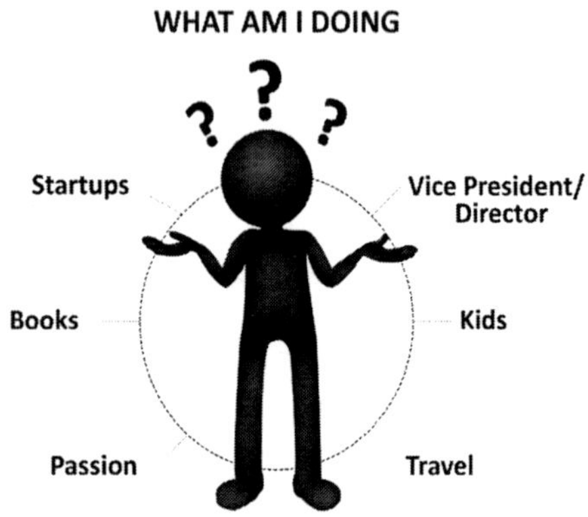

Figure 1: Ron feels he is doing 'not-so-well'

> *Social networks make Ron feel he is doing 'not-so-well' in his own life.*

Comparing himself to this fictitious guy – and since our minds cannot tell the difference between a real experience and a vividly imagined one – Ron feels significantly left behind in the past six years out of campus. He cannot stop his mind from extrapolating this difference over next twenty years and gets totally freaked out. By playing this game, Ron's mind almost always succeeds in putting him into instant depression.

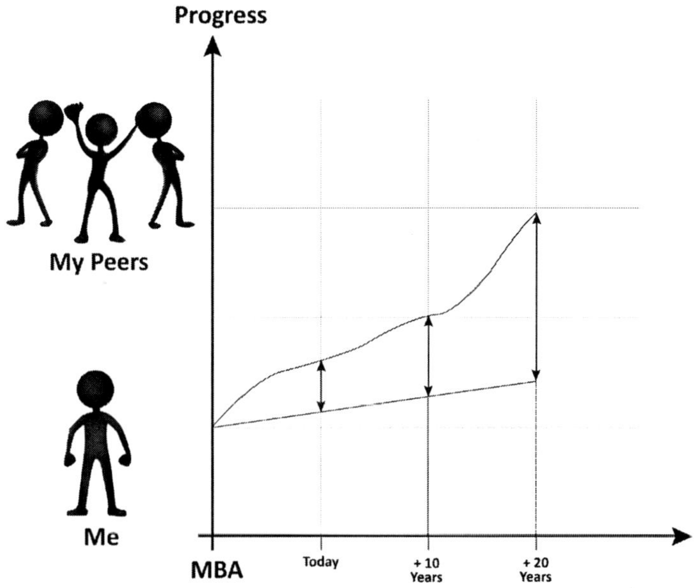

Figure 2: Being left way behind in twenty years!

This feeling has started to bother Ron more and more recently, however, he does not really know how to come out of it. Not having a clear passion and not sure what would be the best use of his time, Ron ends up spending most of his time with his friends who are also in similar situations. All their discussions focus on how they have already been left behind. Ron realizes that having the same discussions over and over with the same people would not bring any results. But, at least he feels understood and feels a strong sense of connection when he shares his troubles with people in similar situations.

Although Ron lives a fairly comfortable life, he feels that something is missing from the entire scheme of things in his life. It is almost as if his expectations out of life, say, ten years ago did not get fulfilled. He feels 'stuck', as though he is still struggling to accept if that is all life had to offer, after all the hard work he put in all these years to establish himself.

Although Ron's life is comfortable, he feels something is missing from the entire scheme of things in his life.

He has many questions in mind about his career, the absence of a clear passion, the absence of a perfect life partner and the overall direction in which his life is headed. He realizes from people though that having a married life, especially kids, creates a lot of meaning and purpose in peoples' lives. He is hopeful that his life might also get a purpose once he finds the 'right' person. He questions himself a lot, discusses these topics on-and-off with people around him but somehow has still not reached any conclusions. On any given day, he can experience a full range of conflicting emotions about himself and his life: sure and unsure, secure and insecure, excited and bored, loved and lonely, fulfilled and empty, impactful and meaningless, all within a duration of just a couple of hours.

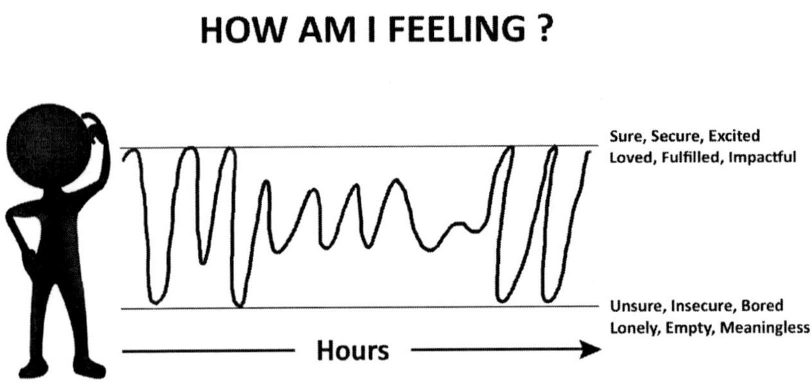

Figure 3: Ron's feelings

Ron is fine with his job, especially since it pays his bills. At the same time, he is a bit unhappy as he feels that he can do more than his job allows him to. He also does not clearly see how far his job can take him. However, he is not too unhappy with it that he will make a change, so continues to live in that in-between zone, more commonly known as the 'comfort zone'. He understands that it is difficult to create anything of extraordinary significance from this zone, however, he is too reluctant to let go of it. Or putting it in other words, between 'fear of uncertainty' and 'boredom and meaninglessness', he has decided to choose the latter, and well, it seems to be the more commonly adopted choice in general by everyone around him.

Between 'fear of uncertainty' and 'boredom and meaninglessness', he has decided to choose the latter, and well, it seems to be the more commonly adopted choice in general by everyone around him.

Ron's health is fine. He goes for brisk walks and the occasional swim whenever he can find time. Health has not been an area that he has consciously focused on so far, but he is increasingly beginning to realize the need to start. This push comes from a combined pressure of feeling the impact of ageing within his own body and the fact that some of his peers are running full marathons – needless to say they publish those pictures on social networks.

Ron's financial situation seems fine too. He is able to afford the necessities while saving money for his future. He bought a house last year, where he currently lives and pays regular mortgage payments.

So what areas of Ron's life did we not talk about? We covered the Physical (Health), Intellectual (Work), Social (Relationships), and Financial (Money). Oh yes! We missed Spiritual (Soul), kind of an important one!

We covered Physical (Health), Intellectual (Work), Social (Relationships), and Financial (Money). Oh yes! We missed Spiritual (Soul), kind of an important one!

Spiritually, Ron always had a strong sense of faith. However, over last few years, he has started to feel lost, trying to find his place in the world. His overall guiding philosophy of 'do good from your side and life will take care of your results' that used to work well till his education, seems to have stopped working. To summarize, we can say that in an uncertain world, his faith does not provide him with an absolute sense of certainty anymore.

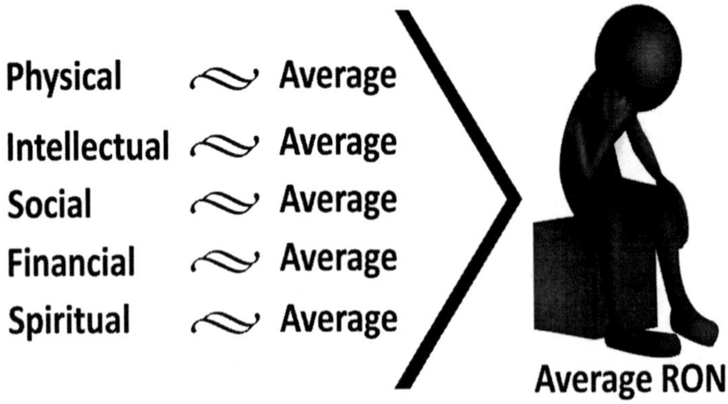

Figure 4: Ron's description

2. THE MAGICAL MEETING

Life moves on, day-in day-out. The questions in Ron's head become louder with each passing day. On one of the days, Ron gets to know that a classmate from his MBA program has resigned from his job and is going to US for higher studies in the area of his interest. For reasons beyond his comprehension, Ron begins to feel disturbed. Since he has always liked his classmate, he is unable to figure out why he feels bad about this news at all.

Ron helplessly tosses and turns in bed with no hint of sleep. He knows this lack of sleep. It happened to him in the past on nights when he was too anxious. However, the frequency seems to have increased considerably in the last few months primarily triggered by new pieces of similar information. In his moments of helplessness and anxiety about his feeling of being 'stuck' and not being able to foresee an appealing future for himself, Ron starts to frantically challenge his faith and pray that some path be shown, to get him out of this life of constantly 'dragging himself' through the days.

Ron is desperate to seek a way out of this life of constantly 'dragging himself' through the days.

In a trance-like state, half-asleep, half-awake, Ron feels a sudden rush of energy and certainty, as if all his prayers have been answered. A gentleman stands before him – who to be described in the least words, would be the ideal version of Ron – smart, elegant, fit, and most importantly carrying a happy glow on his face. Ron recognizes this glow. He used to have it until a decade ago. He is absolutely startled to see this person smile at him. He shouts out loud in astonishment, "Hey, who are you?"

Figure 5: Answering of Ron's prayers

"Ron, I know you are surprised to see me! I was expecting this reaction. Do not be surprised. I am you, five years into the future, from where you are right now. To give me a name, you can call me Ron+! If we decide to call me anything else, then you will start to disassociate me from yourself, convincing yourself that it is impossible to get here!"

> \+ ***"I am you five years into the future, from where you are right now."***

"Ron+! I like that name! I can see that you are quite an enhanced version of my current self, so let's stick to it. What do you do these days, how's your life?"

"My life is excellent! I like my progress in most areas of life and I work hard to maintain and push it further. I wanted to change my job five years ago but decided not to. I changed my attitude instead and I realized that I started to like the same company and the same people more than I ever did before. I stuck around, worked even harder, got two promotions and now handle a fairly senior role for them. On the health front, I progressed with my physical training and have been running full marathons for the last couple of years."

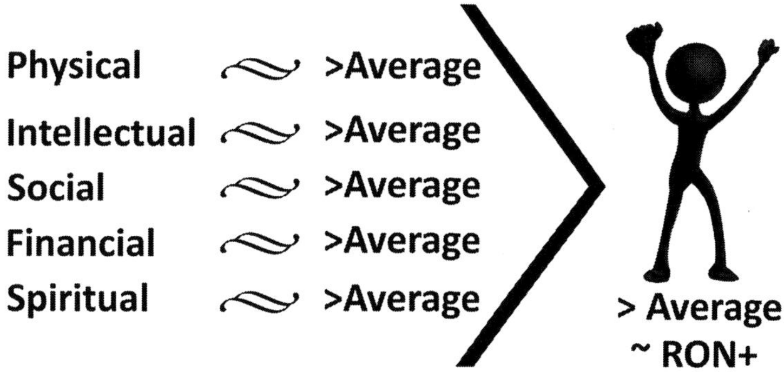

Figure 6: Ron+'s description

"Wow! That sounds great! On the personal front, did you manage to find someone?"

"Yes! I got married three years ago to my 'perfect' partner! She is exactly the one who I always imagined myself settling down with!"

"Wow, that's super! But really, I could have never imagined myself to be ever like you!"

"That's fine Ron. It is quite normal. Most people are unable to visualize their best selves and that is one of the key reasons for why they are not inspired to get there. I understand you have been struggling with some questions in your mind. I am here to help you find the answers. In fact, you have all of them within you already. I will support you in bringing them forth. Let me start by telling you that none of the questions you are struggling with is new. These questions have been around for centuries and the approaches to get to the answers are already well-documented."

> \+ ***"Most people are unable to visualize their best selves and that is one of the key reasons for why they are not inspired to get there."***

"Well, if the answers are available so easily, why do I see many people around me struggling to find them?"

"Tell me this. Ron, do you think wisdom can be shared?"

"Hmm… Not sure, may be not!"

"You are right! It is knowledge that can be shared. That's what I will share with you. Wisdom is more like a Do-It-Yourself (DIY) project. The documented principles can show you the path. It is you who will have to walk the path to get your answers. Every individual on this earth is unique and very different from anyone else that has been here and will ever be, and so are the answers for every individual."

> + ***"The documented principles can show you the path. It is you who will have to walk the path to get your answers."***

"Ron+, how did you become the way you are?"

"It's not rocket science! In fact, rocket science might just be the only thing that is truly rocket science. You can say that I was living a life exactly like yours five years ago, struggling to accept the meaninglessness of the whole thing and having a zillion questions on my mind – the same ones as you have now. And one day, a key insight struck me – 'I was looking for answers in places where they did not exist.'"

> + ***"I was looking for answers in places where they did not exist."***

"Oh! What do you mean? Can you elaborate?"

"Sure. Leading my usual day-to-day life and expecting answers to my questions from the people and environment around me was not the right approach. I decided to make a change in the places I was looking for the answers in, and the people I was discussing my questions with. On my single-minded quest for the answers, I became a voracious reader. I started reading books in self-help, psychology, philosophy, personal development, leadership, communication, mind-body connection, spirituality, and autobiographies and biographies of successful people. I listened to audio tapes, watched interviews, and participated in multiple training programs.

In fact, I tried every source I could, to hear from the people who seemed to genuinely lead more fulfilling and enriched lives."

"Hmm... and what did you find?"

"I confirmed my understanding of the principles and began testing some of the tools and strategies in my own life, and guess what? With consistent application, they seemed to produce results! On a daily basis, what we live are not our lives, but really our habits and patterns. It is estimated that 90% of our daily decisions are governed by our habits. It is perfectly fine to live our habits as they make our lives simpler and we do not need to take every small decision every day. However, the challenge begins when some of the habits that we live, do not serve us constructively anymore. The key then is to identify the habits that are not serving us well and to replace them with the ones that will. It takes a while to build initial momentum, but once you have it, it grows exponentially and you can see yourself transforming quickly across all areas of life. So, to summarize – I understood the principles, acquired the time-tested tools and strategies, began to apply them in my life on a consistent basis and still continue to do that."

+ ***"It is estimated that 90% of our daily decisions are governed by habits. It is perfectly fine to live our habits. The challenge begins when some of the habits that we live do not serve us constructively anymore."***

"So, Ron+, since you know so much, can you tell me how I can find meaning in my life?"

"Wow! You are really eager to get into deep stuff directly. I am kidding! I don't understand why people make such a big deal out of 'finding meaning in life' and go on a search for some 'standard' meaning. My understanding and experience says that we can consider flipping our perspective. We can stop asking 'What is the meaning of my life?' or 'What does life have to offer me?', and instead ask, 'What meaning can I bring to my life?' or 'How can I make this world better with my presence?' The former two are 'receiving' kind of questions while the latter two reflect a more 'giving' attitude. And always remember, the answers we get in life are a function of the questions we ask. Ask better questions, and you will get better answers!"

> ***"I don't understand why people make such a big deal out of 'finding meaning in life' and go on this search for some 'standard' meaning."***

"Oh! What do you mean to say exactly?"

"Well, my sincere apologies if I sound harsh but people all around seem to have massive expectations on how the world should be and how everyone around them should behave. Day-in and day-out they claim that they are feeling stuck, are bored and act grumpy as if life owes them all the comfort, love, joy and contentment. We both know that feeling – you are there now and I been there few years ago."

"Hmm, so what might be a better approach?"

"Why don't we all just focus on becoming our best selves, and as we become more, contribute back by sharing the learnings from our growth with others so that they too can experience the same? And trust me; there is no end to this process. It is already a lot of work to do. It is fundamental nature of the human spirit to long for growth. In fact, the universe is constantly expanding too. We humans feel alive when we are growing. Grow or die is the law of the universe. As Anthony Robbins said, 'Anything that isn't growing, is dying!'"

"People tend to take the feeling of getting stuck and being bored at face value and do not dig deeper to understand where it comes from. In my view, this feeling signals two things (i) all activities that we do in our lives have become too convenient, and (ii) there is too much comfort and certainty indicating that we have stopped growing (or beginning to die!) and that we need to challenge ourselves in newer ways to stimulate growth again. No matter where we are in our lives, there is always scope to go the next level in each of our life areas. And as we grow and expand, we can continue to share the fruits of our success and our learnings with others on the way. Let me tell you about the key life areas to help you structure your thinking."

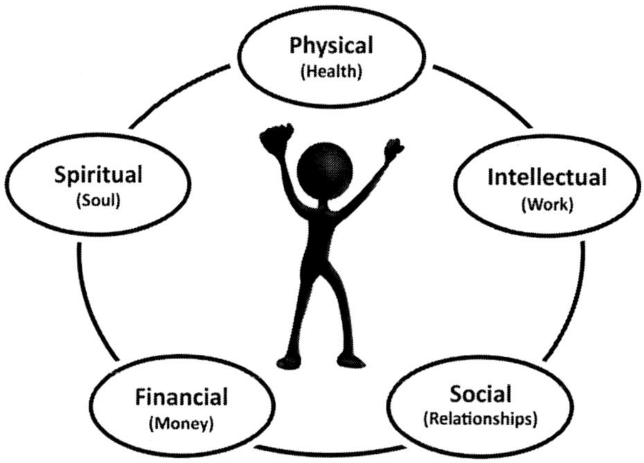

Figure 7: Areas of life: Aspects of the 'I'

Table 1: Areas of life

Life area	What does it cover?
Physical (Health)	Your body and the sense of energy or vitality that you feel on a day-to-day basis
Intellectual (Work)	Your work. It can be a job or business, whatever is applicable in your case
Social (Relationships)	Your relationships, both the intimate one and others i.e. family, friends and acquaintances
Financial (Money)	Your financial standing including your earning potential, savings and assets
Spiritual (Soul)	Your essence of being, your connection with God, the Source, or whatever name you choose to give it

"How about 'Emotional' Ron+… Are you excluding it for a reason?"

"Yes. In some other sources though, you will find it listed as a life area. For me, it is directly impacted by how you are doing across all these other areas. I do not treat it as a standalone area. It is more like the ultimate measure of how you are doing overall. If you consistently feel negative or disempowering emotions, it wouldn't really matter how well you are doing in other areas. Don't all of us want to feel good or feel positive emotions most of the time and that's why we do all that we do in the other life areas?"

"Yes, I see what you mean. These things sound nice, Ron+! But, life is tough. There are unexpected ups and downs that one has to deal with!"

"Ron, I hear you that life is tough, but compared to what? Let me tell you this. Most of our suffering in life comes from just one thing: our assumptions or, say, our judgments, it's the same thing. We want things to show up and remain in the ways that we like. Whenever we do not like what shows up, we call it a 'problem', although it might just be an equally probable outcome of some event. A better practice is to call it a 'challenge'. Sometimes, just by choosing to call something differently, we can start to feel differently about it. We can talk about this in more detail later."

> ***"I hear you that life is tough, but compared to what?"***

"Remember, there is no growth without challenges. How can you experience happiness as happiness if there was no sadness? How can you appreciate a high if there was no low? Would you know white as a distinct color if everything was white? Change is a law of nature and although we are becoming better at predicting it, we still cannot get it accurate all the time. We are constantly trying to create certainty in an uncertain world, however, remember that the only absolute certainty that we can create is within ourselves, it cannot come from outside."

> ***"We are constantly trying to create certainty in an uncertain world, however, remember that the only absolute certainty that we can create is within ourselves, it cannot come from outside."***

"You make sense, Ron+. I appreciate all that you are saying, but trust me, even if someone forced me to visualize myself five years from now, I would not have been able to visualize myself to be the way you are!"

"Ron, as I said, it is well-established that people are unable to freely visualize their ideal best self without a negative influence from their current situation and the views they have about themselves and the world in general. Another effect that operates here is as stated by Peter Drucker when he said 'Most people tend to overestimate what they can achieve in one year and underestimate what they can achieve in five years.' In fact, going by empirical evidence, over a five-year time horizon, even seemingly impossible feats can be made possible. You must have come across the 10,000 hours rule to mastery, 'Once you put in 10,000 hours consistently into something, you tend to achieve mastery in that area'. A disciplined five hours put in every day for five years will get you quite close to that."

> ***"People are unable to freely visualize their ideal best self without a negative influence from their current situation and the views they have about themselves and the world in general."***

"As a starting point for our transformation, we need to visualize our best selves living our dream lives. Only that can provide us with a strong enough 'why' to start making changes to our comfortable lives and keeping at them even when the going gets tough. And do remember that one needs to really let the imagination go free and imagine the best for us in each of the life areas. Additionally, it is absolutely required that we write the goals down as writing engages the motor part of the body as well thereby committing more of the person than just the mind engaging in day-dreaming or wishful thinking. We can talk more about this in the coming days."

"Ron+, I came across some self-help and personal development books and the principles really seemed to be common sense. But when I tried to apply some in my busy day-to-day life, they caused so much disruption. I felt totally overwhelmed, and then I stopped."

"Ron, you are right! The principles are not something esoteric or secretive. They are fairly simple with the real challenge being in execution. Let me tell you some reasons why they might not work:

1. ***Trying them out without fully trusting them*** – Most people are so skeptical about the entire concept of self-help and personal development that they never trust the principles enough. They start to experiment with them but can never really let go and absorb the advice fully. And so, what happens next is something you can very well imagine. Remember

this Ron, half-hearted attempts do not produce half of the results – they produce no results at all!

> + ***"Half-hearted attempts do not produce half of the results – they produce no results at all!"***

2. ***Trying to change too many things at the same time*** – These books typically are repositories of the authors' insights and wisdom gathered over decades of experience. They tend to be quite rich in knowledge and can make you feel that there are hundreds of things that you should do to get the results you want. It is true that there is no single magical strategy that can transform your life overnight. A holistic transformation requires you to work in multiple areas. However, the good news is that once sufficient momentum is created, the progress in each area starts to feed into others. Trying to do too many things at the same time leads to a major deviation from your normal routine, creating so much disturbance that you strongly get pulled towards your initial patterns.

3. ***Having an external rather than internal focus*** – Some more technique-oriented literature, especially the productivity and efficiency type, focuses on encouraging people to use a number of tools and techniques on the outside and change their behaviors, without really making any shifts inside of them. People start but lose momentum quickly as they lack a strong enough 'why' for doing it in the first place.

4. ***Ignoring how people can leverage peer support*** – We are social beings and spend most of our time in the company of other people, that is, family, colleagues, friends and acquaintances. Our peers exert a massive influence on our choices and behaviors. Humans are driven by the urge to 'fit in' and 'conform', and hence our choices largely tend to be a function of our peer group. When people first begin to make changes to their lives using personal development techniques, a strong resistance comes from the peer group. If we can learn how to get the peer group on our side by informing them in advance on what we are trying to achieve and that we would require their support, we can get them to be on our side."

> ***"Humans are driven by the urge to 'fit in' and 'conform', and hence our choices largely tend to be a function of our peer group."***

"And I guess anyone who shows resistance even despite that, should not be in our peer group anyway, right?"

"Indeed! I have seen people who start trying this stuff and when it doesn't work, they adopt a view that, 'this self-help stuff doesn't work!' What they are essentially saying is that, 'this self-help stuff doesn't work for me!' and that is primarily because they did not get the right enablers and environment for it to work. However, what really disappoints me is something bigger. When people try these techniques and are unable to succeed, they lose more than just the benefits they could have acquired from them. Trying something and not succeeding at it tends to reduce our self-esteem, which can then impact us in all areas for the rest of our lives. We can cover much more on the topic of self-esteem at a later stage."

> ***"I have seen people who start trying this stuff and when it doesn't work, they adopt a view that, 'this self-help stuff doesn't work!' What they are essentially saying is that, 'this self-help stuff doesn't work for me!'"***

"Ron, the universe works on laws, some of which we learnt at school. There is one more law that everyone needs to be aware of: the law of intention. There are many authors who write about this. It is unfortunate that most people continue to live their lives without understanding this law. I say unfortunate because the law does not stop operating for people who do not know about it or do not agree with it. The law continues to operate and people continue to produce the results they do not want without even understanding the root cause behind it. Whenever people tell me that they tried applying the law of intention and that it did not work, I ask them, 'Be fully honest, what is it that you felt with more certainty – the desire to have that new house or car or job or relationship or anything that you wanted or the belief that you cannot have it?' In most cases, the feeling of 'not being able to' is stronger than the 'want to have', which inevitably invalidates your expressed intent. We all live with massive contradictions and resistances within us that inhibit the process of manifestation by negating our power of desire to a large extent."

> + ***"Even if you do not know of them or do not agree with them, the laws of the universe apply to you."***

"So, are you saying that we create our own realities?"

"Well, most people typically challenge the assertion that they create their own realities. It is perfectly logical for them to reject it as they do not understand it fully. To clarify it more, I can tell you that people create their own reality but they do it from heightened states of awareness or consciousness. And, since most people hardly ever get there, they are not able to create their realities and hence do not believe in the operation of the law of intention."

"Hmm... Can you tell more?"

"Sure, there is a unique frame of mind that makes creation possible. Let me describe it for you:

1. ***You are fine with what you have in your life at the moment and feel grateful for it*** – Consider this. If you are not grateful about your current situation and feel disgusted with what the law of creation has created for you, how do you expect to get it on your side and create the things that you want for yourself in the future?

2. ***You have clearly imagined what you desire*** – A clear command is quite important for the law of intention. The law of creation responds only to the extent of clarity that is provided in the first place.

3. ***You think and talk in positives*** – The law of intention does not understand 'negatives'. For example, if I ask you to visualize your mom, you instantly picture her. Now, if I ask you not to visualize your mom, you still picture her. Our brain works with images and there is no associated picture for 'not'. So, if you are constantly saying that 'I should not meet with an accident' or 'I should not live in poverty' or 'I should not get sick', then you can very well guess what you are attracting in your life!

4. ***You live in positive anticipation*** – You live with a constant sense of hope that all good things you aspire for are on their way already and would be presented to you at the right moment. When someone asks you a question about something you want, for instance, say 'Do you have kids?' or 'Have you traveled to the States?', you realize that saying 'Not yet' is a better response than saying 'No'.

5. ***You show complete trust and faith in the law*** – There is an element of time lag between creation and manifestation that people do not understand fully. Once the request has been made, we need to carry on with our normal lives without getting impatient, but while maintaining a certainty within us all along, that whatever we asked for is on its way. To manifest in the material world, things require a certain amount of time, for instance, to expect great returns from your business, or to achieve a top position in your job, patience, hard-work and experience are necessary, all of which require time. The key is to not take the delays as denials."

"But Ron+, this optimal creation state that you are describing… I see that it is quite tough to get there!"

"Yes it is… So essentially, what doesn't work for people is not the law of intention, but getting into the creation state. Imagine if you could get the creative force on your side, would it not be a better life experience if you walk with the advantage of knowing that you will end up as a winner eventually?"

"Sure! It seems that you can really help me understand these things well."

"Ron, since our lives run on autopilot most of the time, it is difficult for us to see how we take decisions and their corresponding impact on our lives. The ability to step out and look at ourselves like a third-person would is a key technique for transformation. Living our day-to-day lives of stress, confusion, negativity, and boredom, we create so much mental fog in our minds that makes it difficult for us to think clearly about the adverse impact of some of the things that we do or decisions that we take."

> ***"The ability to take your consciousness out of your body and look at yourself like a third-person would is a key technique for transformation."***

"It is here that we can explain the existence of and continuing growth in the profession of coaching. A coach is typically a person with whom you can be fully honest and this person is readily available for you to have a purposeful conversation anytime you want. As an immediate impact, coaching conversations help you clear the mental fog, regain perspective and make better decisions. As a long-term benefit, coaching conversations help you clarify your vision, adapt your current life for it to be aligned with your vision and goals, uncover your unconscious behaviors and patterns, overcome your fears, monitor your progress and stay focused on your path."

"I am sure you will agree with me on the assertion that most high-performing people work with personal, life, results, and performance or success coaches. Does it not sound counter-intuitive that these people are so successful and still have coaches while you, on your way there, with a long way to go, do not? In fact, a good coach can help you cut some years and considerable pain off on your way to wherever you want to reach."

> ***"Most highly successful people have success coaches. They are already successful; do they need these coaches more than you do?"***

Figure 8: I don't need coaching

"Ron+, you make total sense!"

"Since it is tough for people who are untrained in this, if you allow me, I can offer to stay with you for ten days. I can look at your life and support you through your daily decisions. Ron, success is not about doing more or newer things – sometimes it is just about doing less or fewer of the older ones. I will listen to what you say to yourself in your head and no one besides you will be able to see me. Ron, I can provide you with all what you need, but in the end, it is your journey and you need to own it. All change on the outside gets initiated on the inside first. I am extending my most sincere invitation to you to come with me on this journey. Give yourself the gift of these ten days and then decide if you want to continue or discard all that we discuss and return to your life as usual."

\+ ***"I can provide you with all what you need, but in the end, it is your journey and you need to own it"***

"Sure! Let's do this… I am excited!"

"Great! Let's begin with 'I'… Your journey into Individuality, Inspiration and Intensity!"

3. BEGINNING THE TRANSFORMATION (DAY 1)

Ron starts the day with his usual rituals. He hits the ten-minute snooze button thrice before waking up. He starts by cursing the day and wondering why he has to get up each day for work. He then realizes that he has Ron+ with him, and feels better, as there will be some change to his daily monotonous life. In the shower, he is his usual self, complaining in his mind about how his life is so difficult and how he wishes everything was the way in which he wanted. Ron gets dressed and gobbles down a quick functional breakfast. He rushes to the car pool. Ron+ accompanies Ron in the usual one-hour long car ride that Ron takes to his office every day with two of his colleagues. The three of them take turns to drive others in their cars. Ron's turn is in two days. They greet each other and a discussion starts around what each of the guys did over the weekend. The discussion then quickly moves to all that is not right in their lives. They talk about the economy, their company, their bosses, other colleagues, other friends who are putting up glorious updates on social networks, how their own bodies are getting aged, how fun and carefree their college days were, how life has only been deteriorating since and how the future prospects look exceedingly bleak.

Ron+ quietly listens to the conversation all along. He seems a bit appalled at how a fine discussion downgraded so quickly to a 'complain-and-blame' session that could hardly do anyone any good. On the contrary, it would totally convince them of their helplessness to change anything about their lives, keeping them in the rut, that they think they are in, forever.

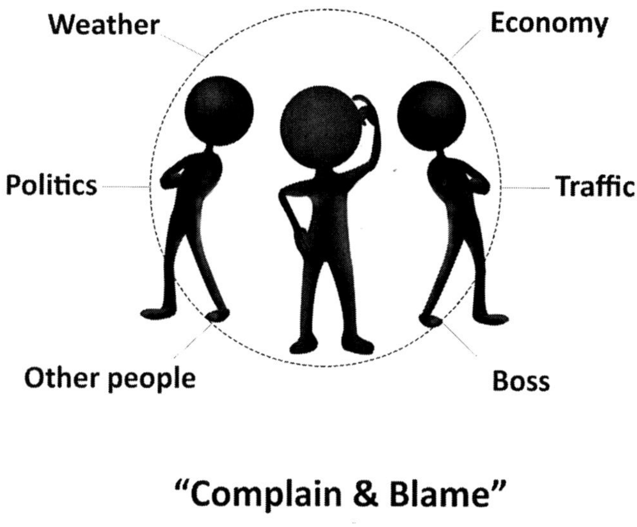

Figure 9: Description of the car pool

There is something for all of us to learn from Ron+ here. Do you think you can listen to three people talk for an hour without you saying a single word?

> ***Can you listen to three people talk for an hour without you saying a single word?***

On reaching the office, Ron practises more of his routine rituals. He greets his colleagues, turns on his laptop, moves to the pantry to grab a cup of coffee, socializes some more there, comes back to his desk, checks email, responds to the immediate ones, flags the ones he needs to respond to by end of the day, updates his to-do list, and marks all that needs to be done that day.

Ron+ seems impressed and thinks to himself, 'Okay, that doesn't seem too bad a start to the work day!'

In close to two hours, Ron seems quite distracted and is constantly trying to multitask working on the presentation for his boss due end of the day, surfing the net to find information for his presentation, random surfing, social networking, chatting with friends on and off, and the constant buzzing of the chat programs on his smartphone, that he is catering to on a regular basis, almost on a 75-25% time sharing basis with his laptop.

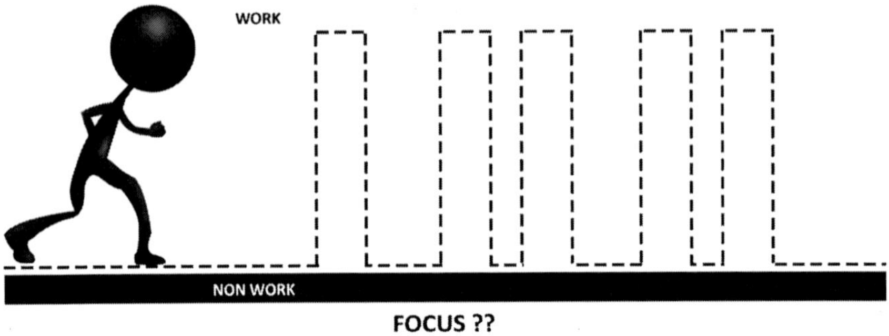

Figure 10: Ron in the office

Ron+ is appalled at how Ron is not engaged in any single activity with full focus. It is time for lunch and Ron accompanies his colleagues to the food court in the office building. The lunch lasts for an hour and appallingly for Ron+ most of the topics discussed are the same as those from the car pool. Although Ron+ is not a trained nutritionist, it was not too tough for him to guess that the group did not make the best lunch choices and also ended up eating more than they probably needed to. Ron+ is sure he would be able to prove his hypothesis in a couple of hours.

Post lunch, work begins again. Around forty-five minutes into checking emails and progressing on work, the group starts to feel low on energy and makes a coffee call. They meet in the pantry, spend another thirty minutes, complaining and talking about how drowsy and bored they feel every day after lunch.

Ron returns to his desk, works for around sixty minutes with full focus, post which he again loses himself in the beeps of his various chat programs. In fact, it is not just Ron. Most of his colleagues seem to be drowned in the constant buzzing of the distracted world that we live in these days. Ron+ is thinking to himself, 'Wasn't technology supposed to make our lives simpler? Or maybe, it holds true only for people who know how to use technology to get what they want rather than being used by technology!'

> ***"Wasn't technology supposed to make our lives simpler? Or maybe, it holds true only for people who know how to use technology to get what they want rather than being used by technology!"***

The nine-hour work day comes to an end. In summary, Ron took a one-hour long lunch break with three coffee breaks each time chatting up with his colleagues around topics beyond anyone's direct control – the usual suspects such as weather, traffic, economy, politics, bosses, and other people in general. It is time to head home. It is not a surprise that Ron has not been able to finish the presentation he had to hand in. He seems relaxed, he knows he is just left with a few minor touch-ups that would take him an hour and he can do them from home at night.

The car pool back home did not see much discussion. There was some minor chitchat, primarily around the same topics. Ron+ remains quiet all along.

Ron reaches home, showers, changes, orders dinner in and pulls out his laptop to finish work. It takes him forty-five minutes to close the presentation, pretty much exactly when the food arrives. He turns on the television and starts to eat. Thirty minutes, and Ron is done, fully available to debrief with Ron+ as they discussed in the morning.

Ron pours himself and Ron+ cups of freshly made green tea as they sit on the balcony for the debrief. Ron+ starts by highlighting certain observations to Ron that are glaringly obvious to an external but not so much to the one living them.

"Let's go to the beginning, as early as the snooze button! Ron, there are two approaches to getting up (i) going straight out of the bed, or (ii) hitting the snooze button on the alarm multiple times. The latter approach indicates to our bodies and minds that we are reluctant to get up and start our day and then no wonder that message sticks with us for the rest of the day. A better practice is to jump start your day by getting out of bed at first sound of the alarm. This can usually be accomplished by placing the alarm clock at a distance where you are forced to get out of bed to turn it off. Once you do that, do not look back at the bed, and go straight into your morning routine."

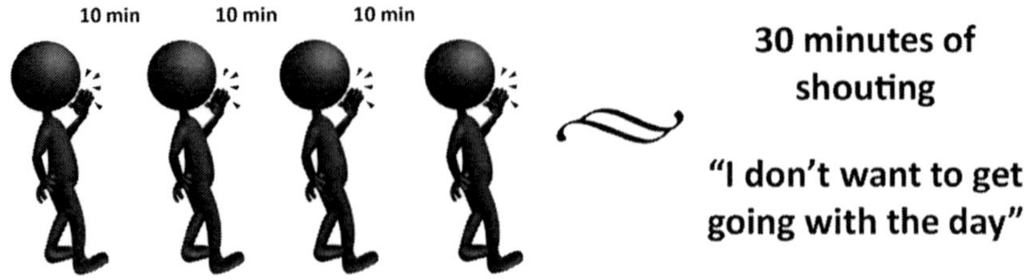

Figure 11: The snooze button

"Snoozing indicates to our bodies and minds that we are reluctant to get up and start our day and then no wonder that message sticks with us for the rest of the day."

"In the shower, you kept talking to yourself in your head, saying how difficult your life is and how you are coping with it. Why would you do that? Look at yourself! You are doing well in life overall. Why would you not want to start your day by thanking life? To just put things into perspective here, I can tell you that almost half of the world, that is over three billion people, lives on less than two and a half dollars a day. You have no idea how many people would be willing to be in your position. I really don't understand why you shouldn't be grateful for what you have."

"Hmm… Ron+, I am grateful in general, just that I forget it sometimes."

"Moving to breakfast… Well, if you can just skip that snooze button habit, you would have thirty additional minutes in the morning allowing yourself to give your body a better breakfast with a more mindful presence rather than just rushing around to put something into your body for the sake of doing it!"

"On the car pool ride, I would like to take the liberty to tell you that I absolutely did not like how you spent your time there! Most of your two hours every day – over a longer time frame, say five years, this would be more than two thousand hours in total – is spent talking about things that you cannot directly control, so it is not the best use of your time. Additionally, focusing on things that one cannot directly control creates a sense of 'helplessness' that further reinforces the feeling of being 'stuck'. The same time can be used to focus on more productive activities such as listening to inspirational audio tapes or relaxation music, reading books, structuring your tasks for the day, typing emails that you can send once you reach office, and many more."

"In the office, you seemed way too distracted, mixing work and play – not the best strategy! Mixing work and play drains out the possibility of achieving full contentment from either. A lot of people suffer from this and do not even recognize why they feel that lack of fulfilment. The ability of human beings to focus on one task is a primary driver for excellence. Instead of honing your focus to be laser-sharp in one activity, you diffuse it across multiple items."

"Mixing work and play drains out the possibility of achieving full contentment from either."

Ron is listening intently, doesn't know what to say. This is the first time someone has shown that keen an interest in his life along with an honest eagerness to support making it better.

Ron+ continues. "I am sorry, Ron, if I am sounding harsh, but you know another reason why most people remain deprived from living their best lives? They cannot muster the courage it takes to be fully honest with themselves about their strengths and areas of improvement."

"No, it's perfectly fine Ron+, please continue… I am totally with you!"

"Great, Ron! I appreciate your courage and am thankful that you are allowing me to give you these strong messages. Most people are so sensitive around this area that they forever lose the opportunity to see the world of possibility that lies beyond these seemingly harsh inputs."

"Most people are so sensitive around this area that they forever lose the opportunity to see the world of possibility that lies beyond these seemingly harsh inputs."

Ron+ continues… "In accompanying your colleagues on multiple coffee breaks, you end up spending much of the office time in more socialization than required. The same time can be used for finishing the work quicker.

Today you ended up bringing work home that you could have easily finished in the office had you been more focused. You could have utilized the time at home for something that added more value to yourself say perhaps a run on the treadmill."

"Hmm, I understand. I never really thought of it that way."

"You have a hobby Ron, and it is not just you, it is something that is widespread across – focusing on things that are beyond our control and feeling helpless. Since we are born and raised in such a culture, it comes to us so naturally and effortlessly that we don't even realize that it is something that we do to ourselves. We practise 'helplessness' and then become extremely proficient at it with years of consistent practice. My best estimate is that people spend around three hours daily thinking or talking about things beyond their control, and probably even more on the weekends. Over a year, it's more than 1,000 hours and over ten years, it's more than 10,000 hours, the time duration in which people can attain mastery in any topic that they put focused effort in. Don't you think you are selling yourself short by not investing this time elsewhere?"

> *"You have a hobby Ron, and it is not just you, it is something that is a widespread across – focusing on things that are beyond our control and feeling helpless."*

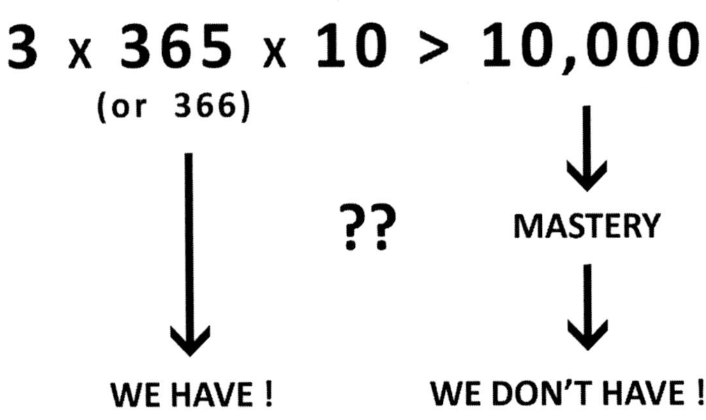

Figure 12: The hobby that sells us short

"I understand... But I do not have a clear passion that drives me!"

"Ron, I think you are making an assumption here. Are you assuming that people who have clear areas of passion actually enjoy what they do 100% of the time?"

"Well, I do assume that!"

"Okay! Let me bring in some perspective here. Yes, it is true that some people are interested in certain things. But what really turns it into a passion is their drive to take massive action towards that. It doesn't mean that they absolutely love every second of it. There are aspects that even they do not like about their work."

"Look at it this way, let's say, every job has two aspects:

1. ***'I have arrived'*** – These are the moments when we absolutely love our work and feel we are at the 'right place' at the 'right time'. These can typically be after we achieve some kind of success or receive recognition from others on our work etc. I am just giving guidance; details can vary by the specifics of the job.

2. ***'Drudgery'*** – These are the moments when we are doing the day-to-day creation of reports or documents, paper pushing, cold calls etc. In essence, these are tasks, we ideally would not like to have in our jobs but from a logical perspective, we can appreciate why they are there. Again, the specifics can vary by nature of the job."

"Now, the ratio of time spent in 'I have arrived' vis-a-vis 'Drudgery' in a normal office job can be say 20-30%: 70-80%. It might even vary within the same job as well, again depends on the job. What is highly unlikely is that it will ever become 100/0%. People in office jobs tend to assume that people who are self-employed, for instance, artists, sportsmen, business owners etc. have this as 100/0%, which is really not true. In fact, if you decide to give up your office job to pursue your passion and establish yourself in that area, the ratio at first will go even more unfavorable from 20-30%: 70-80% to something like 0-10%: 90-100% in addition to the loss of security and comfort of a salaried job. And unconsciously most people know that within, and this keeps them from taking the plunge even if they like certain areas. Yes, with time if you continue to persist and become successful in your area, you might be able to bring that ratio to 40-70%: 30-60%. So, in summary, we have massive contradictions within our own beliefs around this topic."

"You may have an area of interest, but you need to fight for it and be at it despite the initial setbacks. You will not like it most of the time when you start, but overall, once you dig deeper into the area and produce results, you hit the momentum and start to enjoy it more. Keep at it for years and you achieve mastery. It still doesn't mean that you will love every second of it. It only means that you went past the stuff that you didn't like, without stopping."

Interest (small spark)

+ Massive action (hard-work, discipline and making oneself independent of opinion of others especially discouraging ones)

= Passion (sizeable flame that inspires self and makes one come alive)
+ Consistency (continued dedication, commitment and even more resilience for years)

= **Mastery (magnificent light that inspires others)**

Figure 13: The Mastery formula

"Ron, you have a choice. You can either wait for something to drive you or you can choose to bring your drive to something. The difference between champions and others is the ability to continue doing what they are supposed to do even on days they don't feel like it. I absolutely love this anecdote about a legendary violinist. After one of his concerts, he was confronted by a woman who told him, 'Oh, I would give my life to play the way you do!' He looked at her, smiled and said, 'I did!' We will talk more about this mastery formula in the coming days."

+ ***"You have a choice. You can either wait for something to drive you or you can choose to bring your drive to something."***

"Ron, can I change the topic and ask you something along a different area in your life. I am just trying to understand your situation better."

"Sure, go ahead!"

"When you know that relationships bring a lot of meaning to one's life, why are you still single?"

"Well, I have met many girls over all these years, just that I did not find the right one and whenever I did, it was not a mutual click."

"Ok, let's try to understand this! In my understanding of relationships, there are two key rules:

1. To attract someone into your life, you need to either be like them or be like someone they aspire to be
2. To sustain a healthy relationship, you need to give more than you receive

"I don't mean to be harsh but in your case, we can work on both the areas. You tend to like girls who have few reasons to like you in return, leaving you feeling bad and wallowing in self-pity, your helplessness hobby, I told you about. Also, your current level of emptiness does not seem to be a good starting point for a healthy relationship. Most people want relationships to get something out of them and to feel complete. In my view, that's exactly the formula to create an unfulfilling relationship. Remember, two negatives do not add up to a positive. They add up to something even more negative than each of the two individually."

> + ***"Two negatives do not add up to a positive, they add up to something even more negative than each of the two individually."***

"Ok Ron+, so what do you suggest I do?"

"Ron, you have come this far in your life and have done a good job. How about moving to the next level and becoming the person who would naturally attract everything you want effortlessly? It is never too late to become the person you always wanted to be. How about rewriting your life story?"

> ***"It is never too late to become the person you always wanted to be."***

"Sure! Sounds great! How do we start?"

"Great! The first step in the journey from Ron to Ron+ is to get interested in becoming Ron+. You have gotten there, I think. You can visualize your target state and I assume it drives you enough to go through the pain that you will experience on the way."

"Sure, you can say that!"

The two smile at each other.

"The second step is to start living an obsession to improve the results you produce in every life area and enhance its overall quality. This entails understanding the time-tested principles, tools and strategies and implementing them consistently."

"Based on my extensive reading and discussions with people who achieved tremendous success in their lives – and by success – I do not mean material things, I mean overall sense of well-being and fulfilment, I could appreciate the assertion that: 'Our Inner World shapes our Outer World'. This is the single most important insight from the world of self-help and personal development. Every day, while we see more people redefine the word 'impossible', it is ironical how most people still do not practise even the most basic principles from the science of achievement."

> ***"Our 'Inner World' shapes our 'Outer World'. This is the single most important insight from the world of self-help and personal development."***

"We cannot always control our 'Outer World' – Our bodies change, the economies change, people change, ups and downs are a part of life – But what we can almost always control is the meaning we assign to whatever happens. That brief moment between – when we get to know of an event and when we decide what it means to us, is the moment of the 'I' – and that is our free will at play! For most people who are not aware or are not trained at it, this process is so unconscious and rapid that they might even find it difficult to believe that it can be changed. On your journey to transformation, you will have to be actively conscious of this process throughout. We will talk about this in detail in the coming days."

> ***"That brief moment between – when we get to know of an event and when we decide what it means to us, is the moment of the 'I' – That is our free will at play!"***

"Sure, please tell me more about how we can master our inner worlds."

"There are three key areas that we need to strive towards mastering within our inner worlds. The progress made in each of the areas feeds into the others. Once sufficient momentum is created, no matter where we are currently in our lives, we can take ourselves to the next level."

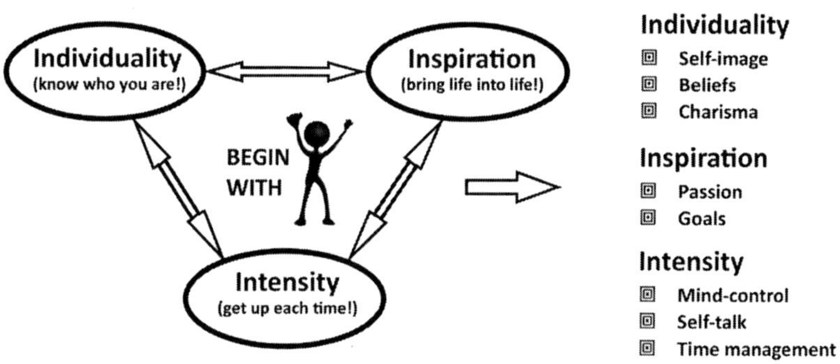

Figure 14: Begin with 'I' framework

"The eight elements within this framework are not new to you. You are already using them currently, just that it might not be in a way that can produce highest levels of joy and fulfilment. In the way you use them currently, they might be in conflict with each other or not fully aligned to function together effectively. Becoming aware of this and understanding specific tools and strategies for each element can help you streamline your energies and become that one invincible force that will achieve whatever it sets its mind on. As William James said, 'Each of us has resources of which we never dreamed.' He claimed that an average individual develops less than 10% of his brain cells and less than 30% of his possible physical efficiency."

"It starts from understanding your own individuality. Know who you are! If you watch people around you closely, you will find that most of us react to situations in predetermined ways rather than assessing each situation independently to decide what is it that we want from the situation. We react based on regrets from the past or fears for the future. The more we understand ourselves, the better we can respond to situations and turn them into becoming favorable to us."

> *"Most of us react to situations in predetermined ways rather than assessing each situation independently to decide what is it that we want from the situation."*

"There are three elements within Individuality:"

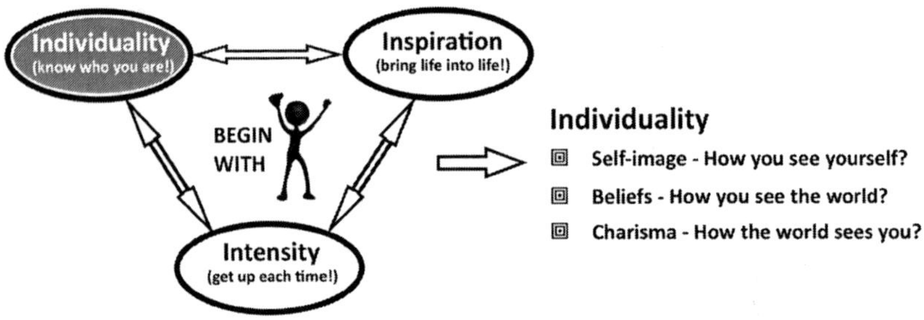

Figure 15: Elements within 'Individuality'

"Let's take the analogy of a car. The elements within 'Individuality' are like brakes, especially self-image. I see people tirelessly pushing themselves to accelerate, still unable to understand why they are not able to speed off to achieve all that they desire. The truth is that most people are driving with their brakes on. This is at varying degrees for different people but most of us have them on. Any small change made in this area will have a significant impact in the acceleration that we can experience."

> ***"Most people are driving with their brakes on."***

"Once you do a one-time assessment of your Individuality, we will work on this together in the coming days, the next pillar is 'Inspiration'. This pillar is about creating larger goals and objectives for yourself, that is, your vision for life. Getting inspired enables us to find the inner strength that is already within us and tap into it consistently so that we can continue to enrich our lives while contributing to others."

> ***"'Getting inspired' enables us to find the inner strength that is already within us and tap into it consistently so that we can continue to enrich our lives while contributing to others."***

"There are two elements within 'Inspiration':"

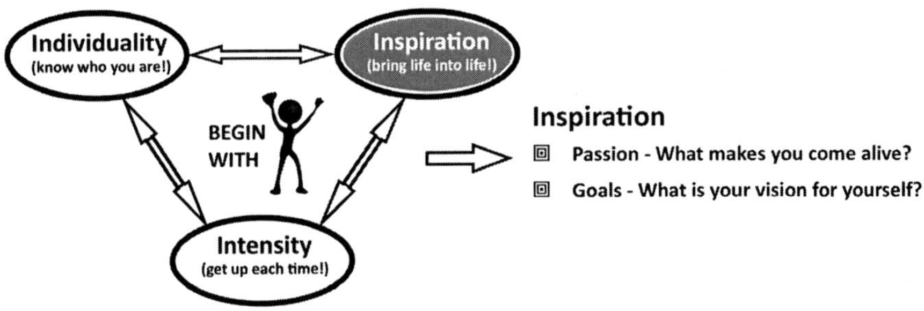

Figure 16: Elements within 'Inspiration'

"In the car analogy, 'Inspiration' is like acceleration. The more inspired you are, the more thrust you feel towards your goals. Inspiration brings 'pull' motivation in your life. It has been empirically demonstrated that 'pull' motivation tends to be more effective than 'push' motivation. Going forward, even the corporates will have to realize this and change their compensation structures. As the nature of work continues to become less routine and more creative, 'push' motivation will seem to work lesser and lesser. If you ever tried pushing yourself to do a creative task with a deadline, you will know what I am talking about. Anyway, we will discuss this in detail later. Let's get back to the framework. This also is a one-time exercise since you have never done it before. We will be working on it together in the coming days. Of course, with time, you will keep updating your goals as you progress along your journey."

"Once you have a realistic assessment of where you are and where you want to be, it is time for execution, that is, time to demonstrate 'Intensity'. This pillar covers the energy and discipline that you can bring to your journey."

"There are three elements within 'Intensity':"

Figure 17: Elements within 'Intensity'

"In our car analogy, 'Intensity' refers to the overall functioning right from the horse power that the engine generates to the harmony with which the various mechanisms coordinate with each other, to enable a smooth and comfortable car ride."

"Once you master these three pillars, you can be sure that you will progress towards the goals that you set for yourself, no matter what the external situation looks like. Sometimes it is favorable, some other times, not so much. But each time, you will acknowledge it as feedback, and not definite success or failure. Life is long Ron, it is a bit like in military – you don't have to win every battle to win the war."

\+ ***"Life is long Ron, it is a bit like in military – you don't have to win every battle to win the war."***

"We will talk in more detail about each of these eight elements in the coming days. I will give you three to four key principles for each element that I have found to be the most fundamental ones. Once you understand them well, you will undergo a shift in your psychology and will be ready for your transformation from Ron to Ron+. As Anthony Robbins says, '80 percent of anything in life is psychology; the rest 20 percent is mechanics'. After discussing the principles, we will work together on some exercises that are quite easy to do even in your busy life and will get you started on the path to your transformation."

"Sure, makes sense. Thank you, Ron+!"

"I hope I made sense! Ron, I don't expect you to start believing all that I tell you right away. I fully appreciate that it is difficult to accept new beliefs just because someone else tells you to. I will give you the opportunity to try them out for yourself and decide how you feel about them. From my experience, I can tell you this – If you apply the techniques well, you will experience life at a level from where you would not like to come back."

\+ ***"If you apply the techniques well, you will experience life at a level from where you would not like to come back."***

With this, it becomes time to call it a day. This time, Ron ensures that he keeps the alarm clock at a good enough distance that he is unable to reach it without getting out of bed.

4. HOW YOU SEE YOURSELF? (SELF-IMAGE, DAY 2)

"Of all the judgments we pass in life, none is more important than the judgment we pass on ourselves." ~Nathaniel Branden

The alarm rings. Ron jumps out of bed, turns the alarm off and launches himself straight into his morning rituals as instructed by Ron+. This time, he is conscious of all that he does and says to himself. He ensures that he is thankful to God instead of complaining. In the process, he realizes how over all these years, he has forgotten all his prayers of thankfulness.

Figure 18: Forgetting all prayers

Now that he has more time for breakfast in the morning, he ensures that he makes it a wholesome and relaxed meal, to give a more energizing start to the day.

In the car, he greets his mates as usual. Instead of explicitly announcing that he will start moving time away from his 'hobby', as Ron+ calls it, to more productive activities, he decides to keep it subtle and gradually make the shift. Ron+ has introduced this strategy to Ron on how he can bring his peers onto his side. The strategy directs people to start making a shift towards what they want and observe how the peer group responds. If the peer group is fine with you making the change, carry on. If the peer group starts to oppose your change, announce openly on what you are trying to achieve and bring them onto your side. Ron buys a personal development classic on his phone and starts to read. When one of the mates asks him what he is reading, he responds saying that a friend of his recommended this book to him. The others acknowledge Ron's response and decide not to bother him for rest of the trip. They continue with their usual discussions, but with lesser intensity than usual, as Ron has interrupted their habitual pattern by choosing a different response. As they don't respond with resistance, Ron decides to continue implementing his change without explicitly announcing it.

> ***"If the peer group is fine with you making the change, carry on. If the peer group starts to oppose your change, announce openly on what you are trying to achieve and bring them onto your side."***

In the office, Ron is conscious about his distracted focus and attempts his best to keep it in check. He realizes that it is not possible to transform overnight but is keen to take at least small steps towards that direction. As Jim Rohn said, "You cannot change your destination overnight, but you can change your direction."

Ron takes fewer coffee breaks, chats less, and completes all the work expected from him with increased efficiency.

In the car on the way back home, Ron again starts to read. He realizes how it had been a long time since he last read a book. He has another major revelation during his reading. In the author of this personal development book, Ron has found someone who is telling him that he can achieve anything he wants in his life if he focuses his mind and actions around it. He realizes it had been a while since someone genuinely encouraged him to become bigger and better and emphasized the need to look at the positive side of things.

In the author of this personal development book, Ron has found someone who is telling him that he can achieve anything he wants in his life if he focuses his mind and actions around it.

He reaches home and since he has no work from office, he decides to go for a run on the treadmill. The run is tough, as it had been a while since he last did it. He comes back home, orders food, showers, watches television for a bit, finishes dinner and starts to chat with Ron+ again.

"Ron, let's talk about the first element within the pillar of 'Individuality', Self-image. We start from here as this is something extremely fundamental to each of us. In fact, everything in our lives revolves around this pivotal concept. Let me introduce you to the key principles here."

Principle 1: Our lives revolve around the concept of our 'Self-image' (yes, I call it a concept as it can be changed!)

"Each of us has a sense of identity that we establish for ourselves over the years. It is the sum-total of our beliefs about us. The core of all personal development and transformation begins from the self-image inside out. This sense of identity gives us our anchor in life and enables us to make all our decisions on what we like, what we do not like, who do we want to associate with and who do we want to avoid. As we mature, this sense of identity keeps becoming more rigid, as over the years, it gets verified again and again. And the simple reason it gets verified is because we always act in ways that are consistent with that identity."

\+ ***"The core of all personal development and transformation begins from the self-image inside out."***

"I don't think I fully get you here, can you please give me some examples?"

"Sure. For instance, someone who is convinced that he is not an adventurous type of person because he met with an accident from such an activity in his childhood will always avoid every opportunity to be adventurous and by mid-age, would have done nothing adventurous at all. If, on the other hand, during his youth, someone had pushed him into experiencing adventure, say a girlfriend or a close friend, someone who had a strong leverage on him – yes, love and friendships provide strong leverages and can push people out of their comfort zones – he might have just liked it and continued onto bigger adventures in life."

"Let me give you a more unfortunate example, say of someone who thinks he is a failure type of person. You can already imagine how rigidly this person would want to live in his comfort zone and how strong an aversion he would have to try anything new. And, if he is absolutely forced to try something new, he will be so full of worries and anxieties that he will actually paralyze his mental and physical faculties into creating the result that is all over his mind, yes failure! And as soon as that happens, he will shout out, 'See, I already told you, I will fail!' Remember Ron, people do not always create the results they deserve, but the ones they expect."

\+ ***"People do not always create the results they deserve, but the ones they expect."***

"Yes, I have observed people living in their own little worlds that they are too scared to make any changes to. Does it have to do something with self-image?"

"Well, with the years, as our exposure in life increases, we come across ideas or individuals who do not necessarily fit into our then view of the world. Given that maintaining a consistent self-identity is a primary need of the mind, the mind immediately disregards these ideas or individuals as things that don't belong to our world. Also, we end up not liking these individuals and it is quite possible that we might not even consciously know why we don't like them. This is when we can know that our sense of identity has started to constrain us. That's the time to make a change. It is not necessary that we forego our previous identity completely, but we can certainly make some additions to it and enhance it further to expand on who we are as individuals."

> ***"Maintaining a consistent identity is a primary need of our mind, even if it means keeping us insulated within our own closed worlds compromising our growth."***

"In fact, if we can go a step further, we should see such a conflict as an opportunity for growth. Isn't it true that people who make us feel uncomfortable, can push us to become bigger and better than what we are currently settling for?"

> ***"Isn't it true that people who make us feel uncomfortable, can push us to become bigger and better than what we are currently settling for?"***

Principle 2: An adequate self-image is a requirement for happy and fulfilling life; to individuals with inadequate self-image, the world can be a frightening place

"Ron, it is well-established that to live a life that is reasonably happy and satisfying, an adequate self-image is a key requirement. It is also well-established now that in case of a person with inadequate self-image, the world can seem to be a frightening place."

"What do you mean by an inadequate self-image? Can you give some examples?"

"Sure, in fact, let me summarize a few characteristics of people with inadequate self-image and I am sure, you would be able to immediately relate to what I am talking about:

- They get jealous quite easily
- They get quite critical and angry when offered feedback
- They tend to take everything personally
- They lack social skills and self-confidence
- They are often uncomfortable when they are alone
- They dress poorly and do not take good care of their health

- They blame something or someone else most of the time
- They spread fear on how uncertain and unfair the world is
- They don't expect much out of life"

"Yes! I guess I know a few people like that. How about the concept of 'self-esteem'? Is it related to 'self-image'?"

"Yes it is. In simplest terms, 'self-esteem' can be defined as the health of our mind. Dr. Nathaniel Branden, a leading authority on the subject of self-image, calls self-esteem to be 'your reputation with yourself'. To relate the two, you can say that someone with a healthy self-image will have a high self-esteem and also higher self-confidence in general."

"Sure, understand!"

"People with high self-esteem are usually strong and secure and can admit that they are wrong when they make mistakes. And to clarify, high self-esteem does not certainly mean that these people will always win. It means that they will certainly give their best in everything they do. These people do not take things personally. As Alan Watts said, 'Angels fly because they take themselves lightly'"

> ***"High self-esteem does not certainly mean that these people will always win; it means that they will certainly give their best in everything they do."***

"Ron+, don't you think that there are more people around with inadequate self-image and the ones with adequate are few and far between. How would you explain that?"

"You can say that! Ron, understand that there are two truths simultaneously operating in this world:

(i) ***It is a basic human need to crave appreciation*** – Numerous authors have been writing about this since ages. As Mark Twain said, 'I can live on a compliment for 30 days'. As William James said, 'The deepest principle in human nature is the craving to be appreciated'.

We don't really need to be a psychologist or a philosopher to understand this. We are humans. We experience it in our lives all the time. We feel good when someone appreciates us for something we say or do. Period!

(ii) ***We live in a negative society that makes it tough for people to develop healthy self-image*** – It is bit unfortunate that the society we live in constantly reinforces our inadequacy more than the adequacy. Most marketing is based on convincing people of the 'issues' with them and how they need to be 'fixed' rather than positive communication around potential opportunities to live more enriched lives. Additionally, the media supports instilling more fear than optimism by constantly highlighting negative news more than positive ones. These tend to create a general philosophy around 'life is a zero-sum game' or 'your win is my loss' rather than 'the pie continues to grow' and 'there is enough for everybody'"

"The coexistence of these truths leads to a rather ironical situation where all people crave appreciation, however, they are not able to give it freely to each other owing to lack of an adequate self-esteem within themselves, thereby creating an overall scarcity of something that is so vital to our existence as human beings."

"Sure, I can appreciate that! But Ron+, people with high self-esteem typically come across as arrogant and narcissistic and are not liked by many people around, isn't that true?"

"Ron, the world in general does not clearly understand the distinction between 'loving yourself' and 'being in love with yourself'. It is essential that people love themselves in order for them to function at their best selves and constantly strive to improve further. Only once you have something with you, can you share it with others. In fact, people are like mangoes, squeeze them and you can only get what's already inside!"

\+ ***"People in general confuse 'loving yourself' and 'being in love with yourself'"***

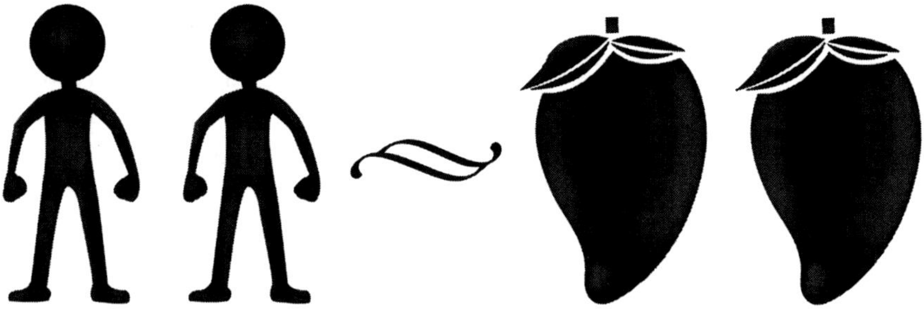

Figure 19: People are like mangoes

"Ron+, tell me more about the people with high self-esteem."

"People with high self-esteem are more open and honest about themselves. They own all their results so there is not much to hide. Also, since they love themselves, they do not like producing average results. So, they push themselves harder each time to get the best results they can. In the process, they discover and begin to appreciate the power of causality, that is, your results are proportional to your effort."

"But Ron+, is it always true that our results are proportional to our effort?"

"Well, it might not always be apparent in the short-term, but in the long-term, yes, it is true. From the frame of reference of these people, talking about results is just fine as everyone should principally own their results. Other people though, who don't own their results and live in 'complain-and-blame' mode, tend to take it as these people being judgmental and impressing their superiority over others. The truth is that once one discovers causality in their life, the first thing they will find to be absolutely futile is spending time judging others."

> + ***"Once one discovers causality in their life, the first thing they will find to be absolutely futile is spending time judging others."***

"When you start to love yourself, that is, you fully accept yourself and are happy in your skin, your temperament towards other people changes. You are always nice to them, making them like you more in return. There is a multiplier effect that gets initiated. Haven't you experienced this on some days when you are genuinely happy about some success or achievement in your life? Or on days when you wake up in an upbeat mood and feel like being nice to everyone around and are more productive at work. You feel good about life and everything it has to offer. It's one of those days when you feel you are in the right place at the right time."

"Narcissism, on the other hand, is being so much in love with yourself that you start to harm others to serve your own interests. It requires a full shift in the value system and can be a case of loving oneself that has been taken to dysfunctional levels. Ron, you don't have to become a narcissist to choose nutrient-rich salads over fast food for your daily meals, or to choose exercising over watching television, or to choose quitting smoking over having a pack of cigarettes a day. We make these choices all the time. Let me not even call them 'better' choices. Let me just say that high self-esteem people make choices that are more aligned with how they want to be. Others though might be wishing for different results, their choices do not fully indicate that, which is then clearly visible in their current situations."

> ***"You don't have to become a narcissist to choose nutrient-rich salads over fast food for your daily meals, or to choose exercising over watching television, or to choose quitting smoking over having a pack of cigarettes a day."***

"Ron+, I feel some positive changes now with social media. People seem to be more comfortable with being open and are expressing themselves more!"

"The world is changing rapidly with significant rise in the level of individuality. The nature of work is moving from more routine to less routine, from more algorithmic to more heuristic-based, from more structured to more creative. This trend started to emerge when we moved from 'industrial age' to 'information age'. In the industrial age, the output per worker could be the same and not be impacted by how the workers felt about themselves. In the information age, as the output started to be linked to individual excellence, individuals with relatively higher self-esteem started to do better as they produced better results individually and were more comfortable in group settings as well."

"From the information age, we seem to be moving into what I would call the 'individuality age' or 'the age of the individual'. People are increasingly finding it perfectly normal to accept themselves more openly. On the work front, the ability to 'quickly act, fail, get up, act again', will continue to become more of a key competitive advantage, bringing increased attention to the underlying quality that makes this competitive advantage possible. And this underlying quality is a healthy self-image. Individuals with relatively higher self-esteem are perfectly fine with continued experimentation and are not scared to fail. They take results as feedback and continue rather than taking them as full and final failure. In this 'age of the selfies' with higher visibility and opportunity to express our individuality, having a healthy self-esteem will not just be a luxury but rather become a necessity."

> ***"In this 'age of the selfies' with higher visibility and opportunity to express our individuality, having a healthy self-esteem will not just be a luxury but rather become a necessity."***

"Sure. This is a different perspective. I appreciate that!"

"On a personal level, the number of options available will continue to explode. Right from what toothpaste to buy to what career to pursue, people will be required to demonstrate more customized decision-making. This can only happen once people learn to move away from the herd mentality and begin to understand themselves and their uniqueness. This requires a high self-esteem. People with low self-esteem will tend to seem more confused, dissatisfied and unfulfilled no matter what choices they make."

"I can imagine!"

Principle 3: We rarely achieve more than we think we are capable of

"Research over the years has consistently indicated that one rarely achieves more than one thinks himself or herself to be capable of. Ron, do you know why most people do not have a lot of money?"

"Not really, tell me!"

"Because they do not feel too good about it and are somehow convinced that they cannot have it. It is the same for our relationships and associations. People usually feel most comfortable associating with people having similar levels of self-esteem. In company of people with high self-esteem, people with low self-esteem typically feel that they are made to feel inferior, when actually people with high-esteem have no such intentions. They are just being themselves. It is the low self-esteem mind that points out the inadequacies in its own self and chooses to feel inferior. A person with high self-esteem is immediately able to recognize that the other has low self-esteem, owing to the excessive neediness and the need for approval that they exhibit. However, they continue to provide the approvals and assurance if they like the person. The person with low self-esteem constantly struggles to believe in the association, wondering how it can be true, so in the back of their mind, they plan to sabotage it to verify their own self-image. With time, even if the relationship is fine, the person with low self-esteem does things, consciously or unconsciously, that would eventually sabotage the relationship."

+ ***"People usually feel most comfortable hanging around people with similar levels of self-esteem."***

"Yes. I can relate to it in context of some people that I have known. So what happens next?"

"The low self-esteem person might be successful in avoiding further interactions with this high self-esteem person and labeling him or her as 'narcissist' or 'self-obsessed'. The unfortunate part, however, is that this reactive response does not do them any good. What happens when the low self-esteem person meets another high self-esteem person? The low self-esteem person again goes into that reactive response and the whole cycle repeats, each time further reinforcing their low self-esteem by sabotaging the relationship. And the worst part is this – at a conscious level, they do not even know that they do this to themselves."

"I understand. What about people who genuinely try to show off their superiority?"

"The cases where some people genuinely try to show off their superiority are in reality, cases of low self-esteem people who develop this as a coping mechanism to find a way to feel good about them."

"So Ron+, what would you suggest is a better response in such cases?"

"A more conscious response would be to objectively assess why you feel inferior to another person. What does that person have, that you would like to have, to be able to be 'natural' or 'normal' around them? Such positive response will serve you well as you will be on your way to increase your self-esteem learning directly from the people who have succeeded in getting what you want. In fact, this is the typical response from a person with high self-esteem. They instantly connect with other people with high self-esteem and instead of getting jealous or feeling inferior, they take the opportunity to seek direct mentorship from them."

+ ***"You can either choose to be jealous of successful people or seek mentorship from them. The choice is really yours!"***

"Yes, I think I have seen similar patterns at work as well, where people with low self-esteem sabotage their chances of moving ahead."

"The same pattern runs in our jobs at the time for promotions. When people within themselves do not feel worthy of a promotion though externally they fight for it, closer to the assessment, their actions sabotage their chances of promotion, even if they were actually going to be given one. At that point, they rationalize to themselves saying, 'I knew that I didn't deserve it!'"

"That is why self-image is such a critical concept and we spend so much time discussing it. Even if we get more than what we think we deserve, we will end up losing it. If we take all the money in the world and divide it equally among every person alive, very soon the money will be back into the hands of the same people who currently have it."

"If we take all the money in the world and divide it equally among every person alive, very soon the money will be back into the hands of the same people who currently have it."

"That is interesting! How do you explain that?"

"I do not mean to indicate that the ones who have the money are cunning or manipulative, but rather, that they are more tuned into abundance than other people. They realize that one attracts prosperity by becoming a certain type of person. A common characteristic of these people is that they always felt abundant even when they didn't have the money they have now. They always felt there was enough for everyone. They first became prosperous in their minds before they attracted it into their lives."

"So, where do you think the issue is? Where do others get stuck?"

"For everything that we cannot do, we have an explanation about how we tried it in the past and it did not work or how it did not work for others and hence it would not work for us. Over the years, we live this explanation. What we fail to realize is that this explanation is the only thing that stops us from achieving what we want. If we can change it, we can change the results we create in our lives. Successful people create explanations that empower them. And think about this: Who do you base your explanations on? Do you base them on people who succeeded or people who could not? Most often, you base it on people who did not succeed. But hold on, did you not want to succeed? How come your explanations came from people who did not? I will tell you why. Because it was convenient to continue staying in your comfort zone and not make the extra effort required for success. We simply adopt explanations that cater to our mind's need to rationalize everything."

"People borrow more of their reasons from people who did not succeed than the ones who did."

"Wow! This is interesting. What can be done instead?"

"Be unreasonable Ron! Set high standards and then go full speed meeting and exceeding them. This is what champions are about. These are the people who bring about a change in the world. As George Bernard Shaw said, 'The reasonable man adapts himself to the world; the unreasonable one persists in trying to adapt the world to himself. Therefore all progress depends on the unreasonable man'"

Principle 4: Our self-esteem is like money in our bank accounts; it increases when we make deposits and reduces when we make claims: The key is to constantly make additions

"At any point in time, we have a certain balance that defines our level of self-esteem. People with low self-esteem are typically so risk averse that they continue to live in their comfort zones so safely that they hardly make any deposits or withdrawals. That is exactly the reason why they continue to remain stuck there. People with high self-esteem are typically risk takers and do things that others fear or they themselves feared till some time ago. These activities continue to add to their high self-esteem. This is one of the potential explanations for why successful people become more successful while people who feel stuck continue to be that way."

"How can one increase one's self-esteem?"

"Although it might seem to be that way, the truth is that we do not gain positive self-esteem by others approving of us. Others approving of us are temporary credits to increase our balance for couple of hours or days or weeks, and then wear off. The only real impact comes from doing things we have deemed ourselves incapable of, so far."

+ ***"Although it might seem to be that way, the truth is that we do not gain positive self-esteem by others approving of us."***

"Now that we are done with the principles, let's work together on a couple of exercises that can be used to enhance one's self-image."

Exercise 1: Baseline your self-image: Things you like about yourself

"Since this is the first time you are doing this, we will establish the baseline. With time, our goal will be to enhance this baseline. Why don't you take some time and make a list of hundred things that you like about yourself? And squeeze them all into one sheet of paper please!"

"Hundred! Ron+, that sounds a lot! I think it's impossible!"

Ron+ smiles, "Ron, you clearly do not seem to like yourself much, do you?"

Ron smiles back. He gets Ron+'s drift and begins to write down his points:

1. I like my education
2. I like my fitness level
3. I like my smile
4. I like that I contribute towards voluntary charitable activities in my office
5. I like that my parents are proud of me

...

...

31. I like that most people in my office like me

Thirty one items and Ron has exhausted all he could think of. "See, I told you hundred will be really tough!"

"You not only told me, you also told your brain that hundred will be tough. No matter how many there actually are, your brain was not going to give you hundred! That's the point of this exercise that you are really stretched to think hard and dig deeper into the many things you like about yourself. You should be feeling gratitude for these things. Now come on and be a sport. Tell your mind that it is possible and direct it to give you hundred!"

Ron starts to write the hundred things down. Ron+ peacefully sits back with a smile on his face. He is seeing Ron struggle to find hundred things that he likes about himself in thirty years of a lifetime. It takes Ron an hour to complete the exercise finally.

"Wow, I never imagined writing hundred things I like about myself would be so tough!"

"Ron, now that you have it in your hand, how do you feel, when you look at this sheet of paper?"

"It makes me feel good! I feel I have not been too bad with my life so far!"

"Great! Now ensure you put this on your bathroom mirror so you can look at it first thing every morning to give a positive start to your day. Remember Ron, our true measure of progress can only come from how far we have come from where we started. It is about how much more we have become. There are no defined starting and ending points in life. Everyone's journey is different, and hence it is absolutely ridiculous to compare yourself to others to measure your progress."

> + ***"Our true measure of progress can only come from how far we have come from where we started."***

Exercise 2: Design the leap to next level: Things you would like to do

"Ron, make a list of twenty-five things that you do not really like about yourself or that you want to but think you cannot do."

"Ah, this sounds bit negative, why do you want me to make this list?"

"As we discussed, the only way to build lasting self-esteem is to do things that you have deemed impossible so far. Two things happen when you do what you deemed impossible:

1. You get a sense of personal victory for having done something you imagined you could never do
2. In the process of doing these things, you exhibit a level of self-discipline or courage that you thought was impossible for you"

"Your self-esteem plays a key role in what you deem possible for yourself. With some of these things done, you can push the limit of your idea of 'possible' a bit further."

+ ***"With some of these things done, you can push the limit of your idea of 'possible' a bit further."***

"That makes sense!"

Ron begins to write. This time he is way faster than he was the last time. Of course, Ron's hobby is to focus on things he doesn't like or he doesn't have. Since it is only twenty-five things, Ron finishes in less than ten minutes. The list looks like this:

1. I want to attract the kind of life partner I wish for myself
2. I feel stuck and bored at work
3. I want to give up my addiction to coffee
4. I can never do adventure sports

...

...

25. I can never do a wildlife safari

"Okay, good job Ron! Now, let us design a leap in your level of self-esteem. We will work on developing a roadmap to do as many of these activities successfully as we can in the next twelve months, but before we get there, a key insight for our way there – we need to travel light!"

Exercise 3: Lighten your backpack: Drop the regrets, they tire you out

"'Travel light' is a common best practice from the lives of people who travel a lot. Nothing tires you out more than lugging stuff that you do not need. Is it not similar to life? Look at people around you. Don't we all carry baggage from our past all the time? Of course there are learnings, but once we internalize them, do we really need to carry the rest of the stuff?"

"Life is all about making choices. We make hundreds of them every day. We made some in the past that did not necessarily give us the outcomes we expected and left us with what we call 'regrets'. If we rank the feelings that stop people from realizing their full potentials and from living their lives at the highest level of richness, 'regret' would be number two, with 'fear' being the all-time number one. As Ralph Waldo Emerson said, 'Fear defeats more people than any other one thing in the world'"

> ***"If we were to rank the feelings that stop people from realizing their full potentials and from living their lives at the highest level of richness, 'regret' would be number two, with 'fear' being the all-time number one."***

"I have some of it and I know most people have it. How can people get rid of this baggage, Ron+?"

"Ron, people move around with these massive assumptions on how their lives would have been drastically different, or you can say better, if they had made different choices back then. Now, they are so convinced that they missed the bus and that there is no point trying anymore in this life. They want to sit around and wallow in self-pity. What they do not realize is that they can get rid of these bags in seconds, the moment they make a shift in their minds. They need to appreciate that they failed at nothing. They just produced some results, which they can consider as failure or feedback depending on how they want to look at it."

"Forgive yourself and life for all that happened. It was a part of your life journey that was essential to give you the learnings you needed to reach this point. There are no mistakes in the universe. The only reason we call them 'mistakes' is because we assigned that meaning to them. Always remember that regret and resentment are like acids, the thing they cause most damage to, is the container that stores them. As Nelson Mandela said, 'Having resentment in your soul is like drinking poison and hoping your enemy will die'"

"Our relationships continue to follow similar patterns as well. Each time, we tend to end up with similar results in our relationships. We are not able to start afresh in a new one as we carry considerable baggage from previous ones and do not give the new person a fair chance to be fully natural with us."

"Ron, let's do another exercise. Write down the five worst mistakes you made in the past, or you can say, five of your biggest regrets in life."

"Sure!"

Ron makes a list of the following five regrets:

1. I did not go to USA to study further
2. I did not start a business after MBA even when I had everything ready
3. I did not accept a great opportunity to change my job into a high-growth industry
4. I chased after the girl I liked and scared her away
5. I did not invest in a house when the market was down

Ron+ again witnesses that it did not take Ron a lot of time to come up with this list. But he is not surprised. Ron+ realizes how it is perfectly fine for untrained minds to focus on the negatives.

"So, how do you feel when you focus on this list?"

"To be honest, I don't feel too good! Although it doesn't happen every day, I tend to be reminded of one or more of these on an on-and-off basis."

"That's understandable. And I also understand what you see as regret now, might have been the best decision at that point in time, that's why you took it. Do you agree with me?"

"Yes, in a way, that is true. More than just me deciding, the overall context somehow was geared towards me taking that decision."

"Now, against each of these regrets, write down two to three good things that happened because of taking that decision."

Ron takes a while and fills out his responses:

Table 2: Ron's regrets and the corresponding good things

#	The decision I regret	Good things that happened due to this decision
1	**I did not go to USA to study further**	✦ I came here and got to experience living in another part of the world ✦ I stayed closer to my family ✦ I don't pay a lot of taxes
2	**I did not start my own company after MBA even when I had everything ready**	✦ I got a chance to travel and live outside my home country, which allowed me to meet people from different countries ✦ I got good work experience that will help me in my business if I want to start up sometime later ✦ I got to make early savings allowing me to invest in some assets
3	**I did not accept a great opportunity to change my job into a high-growth industry**	✦ I continued in my current industry and have been doing fine, with considerable experience, rather than breaking midway to switch careers ✦ Rest, I don't know! I am just assuming it might have been a good opportunity, although without really having done it, it is tough for me to conclusively say how it would have been
4	**I chased after the girl I liked and scared her away**	✦ I have not been able to get over this one. Maybe once I find my right partner, I would be able to appreciate why it did not work out with anyone else till that point ✦ But of course, I learnt a lesson that going forward when I meet someone, I have to be careful about what she expects from me rather than focusing on what I want from her

5	**I did not invest in a house when the market was down**	✦ I used the money to buy a house in my home town which was a good investment ✦ By not committing to this market, I am free to move out anytime I want to

"How do you feel Ron, now that you have written the good things?" "Better, like it was all not too bad!"

"Ron, do you know what my first observation was about your list? Can you guess?"

"I don't think I can! Please tell me!"

"All of these things can still be done. It might not be the same business, job, house or girl, but you can get other similar or even more suitable this time around!"

> \+ ***"It might not be the same business, job, house or girl, but you can get other similar or even more suitable this time around!"***

"Wow! Let me check. Ron+ you are right! I never looked at it this way."

"Ron, you are just 30. You already talk as if the world is going to end. Clearly, you have not been hanging out with positive people. And even if you were 40 or 50, all of these are still possible. Now that you see them in a new light, let's do something that will make you close these negatives for good. Take this piece of paper and physically burn it, like you are announcing to your mind that these topics have been closed for ever and it should not surface them again."

Figure 20: Burning the regrets

Ron does as suggested. In the process, he feels much lighter than he ever felt before.

Exercise 4: Take the leap to next level

"Ron, most people feel that they do not have the courage to do certain things. But when they start doing them, and succeed, they realize it wasn't that bad and in fact, they were able to do them easily. This is the irony Ron! Fear is only on this side. Once you cross over, you leave fear behind."

> + ***"Fear is only on this side. Once you cross over, you leave fear behind."***

Figure 21: Leaving the fear behind

"Now that we have identified these activities, let us create a roadmap to accomplish them in the next twelve months. To do that, I have classified your activities into the following four groups:"

Table 3: Activities to enhance Ron's self-image

Group	Description	Items that the activities will address
Group A	**Activities you can do in the next month**	✦ I want to give up my addiction to coffee ✦ I feel stuck and bored at work ✦ …
Group B	**Activities you can do in the next three months**	✦ I can never do adventure sports ✦ …
Group C	**Activities you can do in the next twelve months**	✦ I want to attract the kind of life partner I wish for myself ✦ I can never do a wildlife safari ✦ …
Group D	**Activities that can take longer than twelve months**	✦ --

"Well, in your case, since you do not have a goal saying you want to win a triathlon or something, we don't have anything for group D. Agree?"

"Sure, fair enough!"

"Let's look at your items in group A first:

✦ ***I want to give up my addiction for coffee*** – Take tomorrow as your last day with coffee. Have as much as you want! We will create a plan for you to quit coffee for fifteen days at least, and then you can decide if you want to continue or get back to coffee. Fifteen days is nothing in your entire life, so it shouldn't be a big deal! Trust me, you won't die!

> + ***"Fifteen days is nothing in your entire life, so it shouldn't be a big deal! Trust me, you won't die!"***

- ***I feel stuck and bored at work*** – For this, we can do two things. First, as we do more sessions in the coming days, you will be able to change your perception of your job. I suggest you keep this one open and start work on it in two weeks. Second, once you are able to view your job in a new light, you will find it easy to work on aspects such as how to spend more time on activities you find meaningful and fulfilling and less time on activities you feel drain you of your energy or are not the best use of your time. Try either of the following with these activities, as it seems most feasible in your context:
    - Eliminate them altogether if possible
    - Automate them
    - Delegate them"

Next, they look at group B and create a plan for Ron to start off with adventure sports, particularly with the easier ones within three months and then gradually move to tougher ones within twelve months. The same exercise is repeated for group C.

"Ron, as you keep conquering these things one by one, you will start to experience an increase in your overall self-esteem. It will continue to grow exponentially and you will be amazed at your progress. You will look back and wonder why you were stuck there for so long, feeling grateful that you started, realizing that it was only the first steps that were the toughest to take."

> ***"You will look back and wonder why you were stuck there for so long, feeling grateful that you started, and realizing that it was only the first steps that were the toughest to take."***

Exercise 5: Once this iteration becomes natural, start all over again

"Once you get done with this list, the overall objective is to keep adding new activities to your life to continue enriching your self-image."

"Doing affirmations also helps enhance one's self-image. You can continue to do them throughout, in addition to the exercises. Out of the two options of saying them in the mind or saying them out aloud, I suggest you make time to do the latter, unless you absolutely cannot, owing to your contextual constraints. Saying affirmations out loud does two things at the same time: (i) you say something you typically don't say to yourself and (ii) you hear something you typically don't hear. It is like reprogramming your mind and body with new information. Yes, body too, as you are using your physical muscles when you say them aloud!"

> ***"Saying affirmations out loud does two things at the same time: (i) you say something you typically don't say to yourself and (ii) you hear something you typically don't hear."***

"Ron, with this, we have come to close of the first day where we discussed Self-image, the first element within Individuality. This was a long session with elaborate exercises as this is the most critical element in anyone's transformation. Even a small improvement in this element creates a ripple of positive impacts across all life areas."

"I fully understand! Thank you, Ron+!"

5. HOW YOU SEE THE WORLD? (BELIEFS, DAY 3)

"It's the repetition of affirmations that leads to belief. And once that belief becomes a deep conviction, things begin to happen" ~ Muhammad Ali

The alarm rings. Ron jumps out of bed, turns off the alarm and launches himself straight into the morning rituals as instructed by Ron+. Although this is the second day, it still does not feel natural and Ron has to drag himself out. However, he has already been made aware that it typically takes around three weeks for human beings to firmly establish a habit, so he is fine pushing himself at this point.

> ***It typically takes around three weeks for human beings to firmly establish a habit.***

On one end of the bathroom mirror, Ron has the list of things he is happy about in life. He starts reading them as he brushes his teeth and starts to subconsciously feel good and resourceful to handle the challenges that this day might present. He has already handled critical challenges in the past.

In the shower, Ron feels grateful about all the good things he has in life. It feels less strange than it did the day before. If we look at our lives and write down what we are happy about, we will realize that more than 90% of the things about our lives are going right. We somehow just choose to focus on the 10% that are not.

If we look at our lives and write down what we are happy about, we will realize that more than 90% of the things about our lives are going right. We somehow just choose to focus on the 10% that are not.

It is Ron's turn to take his car. The car pool seems to have evolved to a less negative and more constructive experience. They start with greetings and quickly get into their own business. One is busy reading. The other is listening to music that would charge him up for the day.

It is usual routine in the office. Ron works with a sense of urgency and ensures that most of his office time is utilized for productive work. Ron is aware that today is his last day with coffee before he switches to green tea from next day onwards. He is aware of Ron+'s strategy about the peer group – 'get them on your side if they resist; if they don't, use your discretion to inform them or not of your new choices.'

The car pool on the way back home is quiet with the radio playing and the guys relaxed. At home, Ron follows his routine. He heads to the gym for a run on the treadmill. The run is still tough, but Ron knows he will start feeling fine over the next few days. He comes back home, orders in dinner, showers, watches television for a bit, finishes dinner and it is time for the chat with Ron+ again.

"Ron, today we will talk about the second element of Individuality, Beliefs."

Principle 1: Our beliefs are the glasses through which we view the world and life (yes, calling them glasses to emphasize that they can be changed too!)

"In addition to the beliefs we have about ourselves that we covered within self-image, we all have beliefs about the world and life in general. These beliefs define the frame of reference from where we view the world. As Stephen Covey said, 'We see the world, not as it is, but as we are—or, as we are conditioned to see it.'"

"If we examine our beliefs closely, we will realize that most of them come from our family, schools and the society in general. We did not really question or test them for ourselves. Most people do that as it is easier to take an established idea and believe it, rather than question and verify it for ourselves. Over time of behaving in accordance with our beliefs, we get massively conditioned to act in certain ways."

> + ***"Over time of behaving in accordance with our beliefs, we get massively conditioned to act in certain ways."***

"As Mark Twain said, 'The trouble with the world is not that people know too little, but that they know so many things that ain't so.' He was referring to beliefs that people continue to have without understanding where they came from. Just think about it – What if just some of your beliefs were not true and have been stopping you from unleashing your highest potential and living your best life?"

> + ***"What if just some of your beliefs were not true and have been stopping you from unleashing your highest potential and living your best life?"***

"Ron, do you know how fleas are trained?"

"Not really. Tell me about it."

"They are put into a jar with a lid. They jump up, hit the lid over and over again. With time, something interesting happens. They continue to jump, but no longer high enough to hit the lid, so you can say they become conditioned to have a ceiling there. Even if the lid is removed, the fleas continue to jump to same height. At this point, someone looking at the jar can safely assume that the fleas are incapable of jumping high enough to get out of the jar. But that is not true at all."

"This was still a situation where the fleas experienced the lid themselves. Let me give you another anecdote. Five frogs are put into a box with an open top. Each time a frog tries to jump out, it is hit hard on its head with a stick. All the five frogs try it once, get hit and then stop trying. Now, one of these frogs is replaced with a new one. As soon as the new one joins, the other four inform it that it should not try jumping as it will be hit hard on the head. The new one does not even try. Then, in some time, one of the other four original ones is changed with a new one. The same situation repeats, the new one does not even try to get out. With time, one by one, all the original five frogs are removed and we reach a situation where there are five frogs, none of which has had the first-hand experience of being hit, but all believe that they will be hit. None of them even tries to get out. This is how beliefs are passed from one generation to the other. People carry them without understanding where they came from."

"That makes sense!"

"You will understand more when we do the exercises. We will work on a few of your beliefs in detail and demonstrate how you have always been acting in accordance with them."

Principle 2: Beliefs are self-fulfilling prophecies

"What I will say now may sound weird. But, trust me, it is true and I hope you can appreciate it after our discussion. Whatever beliefs you hold, will prove them to be true."

> ***"Whatever beliefs you hold, will prove them to be true."***

"Really, can you tell me more?"

"Ron, we live our beliefs and since we always act in accordance with them, we receive the results that we expect. This is how our beliefs become our 'facts'. This is the reason why it is difficult to make people change their beliefs. Everyone's life turned out to be in direct correlation to their beliefs. If someone believed that they controlled their life, they would have acted consistently with this belief, making it come true. If someone believed that their life was controlled by circumstances, they used that philosophy to explain every event in their life thereby assuming a position of lack of control and reinforcing it each time."

"Let me get into some technical details on how this happens. We have five key input channels on how we receive sensory data from the world around us."

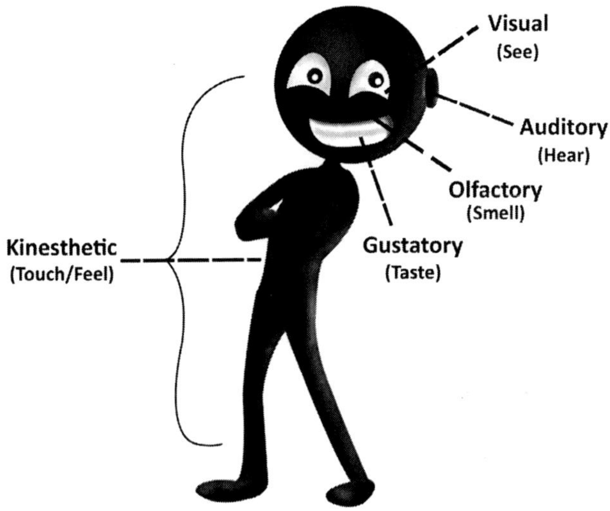

Figure 22: How we receive sensory data?

"It is established that every second, there are close to two million bits of sensory data around us that are trying to enter into our conscious and unconscious mind, thereby making it critical to decide what information is important and should be brought into 'conscious' and what can be made to disappear into the 'unconscious'. This is where our 'reality' is created and is different for every individual."

> + ***"This is where our 'reality' is created and is different for every individual."***

"Our Reticular Activating System (RAS) serves as the control center. It uses three brain processes or filters to go from two million bits of information per second down to five to nine chunks of information, so we can make sense of the information. These processes are: Generalization, Distortion and Deletion. Now hear this out, this is important! In order to filter-in or filter-out this information, RAS uses certain inputs:

- ***Our self-image*** – Our concept of who we are, what are our values, what we stand for, and what we are capable of doing and not doing
- ***Our beliefs, values and prejudices*** – Our concept of what is right and wrong, what we are allowed to do and what we are not, what is good for us and what not so much
- ***Our past experiences and memories*** – Our concept of what has happened in the past. But here again, remember that our self-image and beliefs played a key role as they forced us into having the outcomes that were aligned with them. Most of the memories we recorded or chose to not record from the past events as per our interpretation of them, were already colored by and consistent with our self-image and beliefs
- ***Our patterns*** – Our usual day-to-day rituals that we run
- ***Our survival needs*** – Of all the requirements, our subconscious and unconscious minds place the highest importance on survival as this is the most key function ingrained in them"

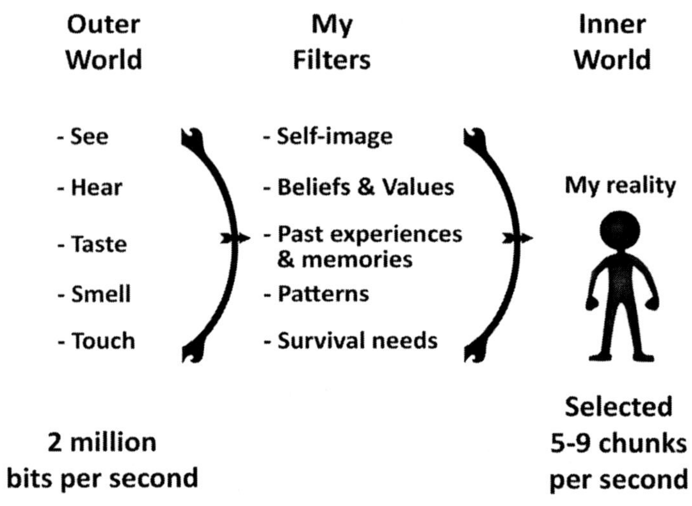

Figure 23: How we create our reality?

"Now, the only pieces of information that we allow into our inner world, that is, our reality are the ones that are aligned with our filters. Any major changes to our filters start to create new realities for us by allowing in new kind of information that has always been out there but we hardly ever perceived it. The more certainty with which we believe something, the more strongly our brains find information to prove it that way. Extending it, the more certainty with which you imagine you can do something, the more strongly your brain will find ways to get it done. Unfortunately, the same holds true otherwise as well."

> + *"The more certainty with which we believe something, the more strongly our brains find information to prove it that way."*

"In a way, you can say that the quality of your life is determined by the quality of your beliefs, especially the fundamental ones that determine your overall perspective. As Albert Einstein said, 'The most important decision we make in our lives is to decide if we live in a friendly or a hostile universe'. Your approach to life will be different if you consider you live in a friendly universe where everything happens for your good, or if you are certain that the universe is out there to get you and you need to constantly safeguard yourself and your possessions. Another way to look at it is what you believe life is all about: Is it a journey, a celebration, a suffering, a trial or something else? Whatever you believe, you will act accordingly, producing corresponding results."

"Some of our primarily beliefs that act as our anchors in life are the ones we have about the source or the higher power or the infinite intelligence or the life force or God. People use different names. The extent of faith or fear you exhibit in life is derived from these beliefs. I refer to faith and fear together as they really are opposite extremes of the same thing. Faith is guided imagination giving us strength while fear is unguided imagination taking our strength away."

> + *"Faith and fear are opposite extremes of the same thing. Faith is guided imagination giving us strength while fear is unguided imagination taking our strength away."*

Principle 3: We can significantly improve the quality of our lives by adopting more empowering beliefs

"Most people in their normal lives never venture into a belief assessment exercise as it can be painful. It is like questioning the core of a person. This exercise can help categorize our beliefs into the ones that empower and ones that disempower us. But the good news is that sometimes, just by recognizing a limiting belief, you can take its power away. For example, if you could adopt the following belief as your most primary belief on life, 'Life doesn't happen to you, life happens for you' and consistently live in positive expectation, you will see that whatever happens, will be for your good. Your approach to life will become optimistic and your overall well-being will improve."

"Let's do the exercises to assess your beliefs about the world and life. This principle will become clearer then."

Exercise 1: Baseline your beliefs: Make a list of your key beliefs and assess how they have impacted you all these years i.e. categorize them into empowering or limiting beliefs

"Since this is the first time you are doing this exercise, it will be kind of baselining for us. Let us look at your existing beliefs and classify them into empowering, neutral and limiting beliefs. Our overall objective is to take most of your limiting beliefs and replace them with empowering ones."

Ron starts to think and comes up with three of his key beliefs. He also writes how he feels about them these days.

1. *There has to be some meaning to life* – I have still not found out mine
2. *Just keep doing good from your side and good things will happen to you* – This doesn't seem to work for me anymore now
3. *To be more successful rather than just having good things, luck needs to play a key role in a person's life* – This is seeming to be more true by the day

"Fair enough Ron. Let us look at each of your beliefs closely and see how it has been impacting you."

"There has to be some meaning to life – This belief sounds worse than an assumption. Here you have passed a verdict that there absolutely is a meaning and you are troubled since you have not found yours. A lot of pain that you have been experiencing in the past months is because of this belief as it triggered the questioning and you started feeling unanchored in life. If we can replace this belief with something that gives you a stronger anchor to live your life with, you will immediately feel more sorted out."

"Ron, life is imperfect. The moment we accept this, our view on life changes dramatically. I don't mean imperfect in a negative sense. What I mean is that there is always something missing. That's how we can know 'perfection'. I do not encourage comparing with other people as no matter how much you see, you will never have enough information about how their life truly is. You will really be comparing their highlights to your behind-the-scenes'.

> ***"If you compare your life with others, you will really be comparing their highlights to your behind-the-scenes."***

"If you have more information than you currently have, you will find that though it might seem like there are people who have everything going right for them, when you look closer, there will be some things missing. If they strive to get those things, some other things will slip away. It is this quest for perfection that makes the human spirit grow. There is always an option to give up on some things and be content with average results in some areas, rationalizing that you were not destined to have good results there. Most people around have done that and are living with their compromises. An alternate approach is to continue striving. Things will slip away and you will have to come back to them, but your level of the game across all life areas will keep improving."

> ***"It is this quest for perfection that makes the human spirit grow."***

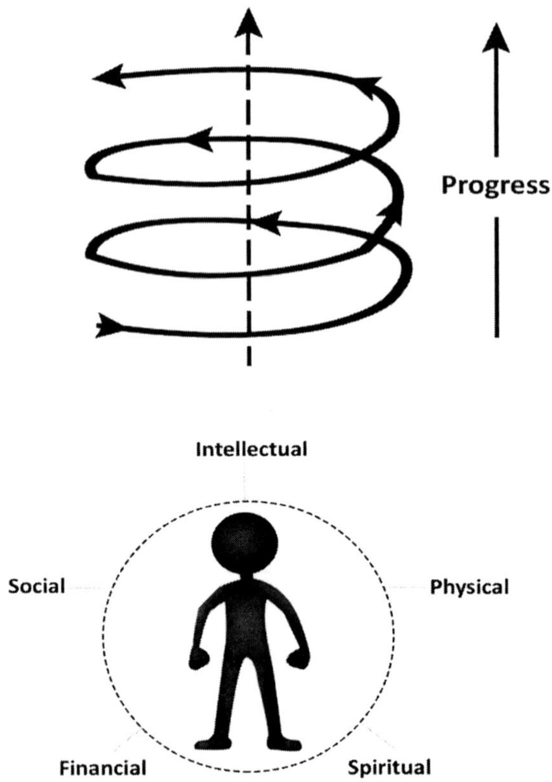

Figure 24: Raising level of the game

"Life is a process, Ron. It is a verb and it is happening. As Albert Einstein said, 'Life is like riding a bicycle. To keep your balance, you must keep moving'. You can never assume that life has gotten perfect and that you can choose to stop moving. It is like doing the Rubik's cube. Once you think you have a few faces done and try to do others, the ones you did go away. And in fact, if you don't act on life, life has its own way of acting on you. What feels like minutes, turn into hours, days, weeks, months, and years. Before you realize what happened, life can be gone leaving you regretful on how you should have lived more than you did."

> \+ ***"Life is a process, Ron. It is a verb. It is happening. If you don't act on life, life has its own way of acting on you."***

"Once you accept imperfection, you will begin to see perfection in the imperfection, and how the whole thing might just have been designed for growth of the human spirit. Spiritual wisdom, through the ages, suggests that the purpose behind some events will always remain beyond our understanding. It is the ultimate test of our faith that we accept these unconditionally without even fully understanding them."

> \+ ***"Once you accept imperfection, you will begin to see perfection in the imperfection."***

"Seasons change. There cannot be sunshine all the time but we can ensure that we take our sunshine with us wherever we go. If life was perfect, there would be no scope to seek perfection in ourselves. Only when life is imperfect, humans get to grow and understand their powers. Ron, remember that enlightenment does not happen despite this world, it happens because of it."

"That makes sense Ron+. I agree with you!"

"Let's move to your second belief now."

"Just keep doing good from your side and good things will happen to you – This seems a good belief to have. It establishes causality. I am disheartened to hear that you are losing faith in it. Let's look at why it is happening. Tell me why specifically do you think this is not working anymore?"

"Despite all the good that I am doing, I am not getting excellent opportunities!"

"Ron, I don't mean to be harsh and you might not like what I will say next. I will still say it, as I know it will help you once you get over the immediate pain that it will cause. As I said before, most people choose to remain average throughout their lifetime as all self-development starts with being honest with one which takes massive amount of courage."

> ***"Most people choose to remain average throughout their lifetime as all self-development starts with being honest with one which takes massive amount of courage."***

"Ron, we live in a mediocrity culture where 'average' is the acceptable standard. To keep their peer group, people end up choosing inefficient and unhealthy habits. At work, especially in the first few years, people significantly compromise on their own learning simply because they do not want the bosses to get credit for their work. Are they not selling themselves short? People do not invest in their development if their company does not send them to conferences or industry events. What we do not realize here is that companies can give us jobs, but it is us who need to be really taking responsibility for our careers."

"We celebrate individuals who break the false ceiling of mediocrity and are able to fly high into the realms of excellence. I am using standard metaphors that the world uses to make you understand what I mean. But what is really happening with these individuals is not that they are going physically higher into the world. They are actually going deeper within themselves to find what is there that can be used to make a difference to the world and people around them."

"Ron, you worked hard in your early years to get to where you are today, but look at yourself now. You are extraordinarily average, you know that and that is scaring you deep down."

> ***"You are extraordinarily average and that is scaring you deep down."***

"Maybe you are right. I feel I am losing the edge!"

"So just change it. It is really that simple!"

"The truth is that you stopped investing in yourself over the past years and began to cash out on your situation. If you start investing again to go from average to extraordinary, you will see that your belief still works."

"***To be more successful rather than just having good things, luck needs to play a key role in a person's life*** – I do not believe this to be fully true. Even if it was, I do not see how keeping this belief can be of use to anyone. It takes the power away from people. Our minds are brilliant at rationalizing the events around us. The challenge is that the rationalization always happens within our current frame of reference and so keeps us confined within our current understanding of the world without letting us grow. In your case, as your mind started to get convinced of the causality belief not working anymore, there was a need for rationalization and thus a belief that would provide your mind with the comfort that it is possible to not have full control over things. Bringing in the 'luck' factor through this belief seemed like a good solution."

+ ***"Even if it was true, I do not see how keeping this belief can be of use to anyone. It takes the power away from people."***

"I do not agree with this belief. I am yet to see a person who applied all the success principles consistently, who was well-prepared and decided not to stop until they achieved what they wanted and the only thing that stopped them from achieving their goals was luck. In fact, if you ask them, they would know what exactly did not work. Successful people always quote luck to equal preparation and opportunity. A certain level of preparation is necessary to even identify something as an opportunity. For example, if I do not have much knowledge of the financial services industry, I do not keep myself up to date with latest trends through reading about them, and I do not network with people from that industry, how can I expect to know if something is an opportunity in that industry? There is no scarcity of opportunities Ron. What is scarce is adequately prepared people to spot them and have the courage to take the plunge to pursue them."

> ***"There is no scarcity of opportunities. What is scarce is adequately prepared people to spot them and have the courage to take the plunge to pursue them."***

"I apologize if I hurt you with anything I said here. As I already said, challenging peoples' beliefs is a tricky exercise as they have been true for them and people have no reason to believe that they were not true. In any belief discussion, the point is not to check if the belief is true or not, but to check if the belief is serving them well or not."

"Although here we did it for just three of your key beliefs, this exercise can be done for any number of beliefs and is quite powerful in helping one see the causality between the results one produces and the beliefs one holds. With this, let's go into our next exercise."

Exercise 2: Design the leap to next level: Discard disempowering beliefs and replace them with empowering ones

"Once your beliefs have been critically analyzed, it is time to discard disempowering ones and adopt a new set of empowering beliefs to replace them. I have indicated my view on what you can do with your three beliefs that we discussed.

1. ***There has to be some meaning to life*** – You can consider replacing this with 'The meaning of life is to see the perfection within the imperfection by accepting it fully' or to make it more personal, 'The meaning of my life is to become the best version of myself, so I can live an enriched life while contributing back.'
2. ***Just keep doing good from your side and good things will happen to you*** – As we discussed, once you increase the input in your life, your output will correspondingly increase, restoring your faith in this belief
3. ***To be more successful rather than just having good things, luck needs to play a key role in a person's life*** – You can consider discarding this belief as this takes the power away from you. If you want to replace it with a more positive one or to build positive expectancy, you can say, 'To be more successful rather than just having good things, one needs to go beyond and give more than just good'"

"Ron, please understand that you do not have to do exactly as I am saying here, you are free to repeat the exercise on your own. The objective is to choose beliefs that empower you rather than disempower you. To give you another example, I have a friend who has a core belief that there is no justice in the world. I really respect him for who he is and the way he leads his life, but we can all see that he is selling himself short. He is capable of putting in an effort of 100%, but he puts in only 20% as he is convinced that even if he gives 100%, it will not be reciprocated."

> ***"Choose beliefs that empower you rather than disempower you."***

"The disturbing thing is that this belief acts like the anchor that keeps a boat stuck on the shore. This belief keeps him from starting. If he is able to change this belief, he will give in 100% which will trigger two things (i) he will experience the joy and satisfaction that comes from giving one's 100%, and (ii) the world around him, including his job, family and social circle, will benefit from this 100% which will get rewarded with both tangibles and intangibles. We are talking of one person. Imagine if there are only one million people in the world who hold this belief. What a loss to the world that this one belief is causing!"

Exercise 3: Take the leap to next level

"Ron, once you identify your new beliefs, it is time to internalize them. Two effective ways to do this are:

1. Write down and stick them at a place you can easily see them
2. Make affirmations out of them and say them out loud. As already indicated, saying out loud is more effective as it engages the physiology and senses rather than just repeating them in the mind"

Exercise 4: Once this iteration becomes natural, start all over again

"On an ongoing basis, as we live our lives, we continue to come across new ideas and people. As discussed, average people continue to discard new information that is inconsistent with their existing beliefs, but not you. You will be open to change your beliefs in order to grow and reach your highest self. Agree?"

"Yes, sure, I will do that!"

6. HOW THE WORLD SEES YOU? (CHARISMA, DAY 4)

"It is absurd to divide people into good and bad. People are either charming or tedious." ~ Oscar Wilde

The morning rituals seem to have been streamlined with Ron getting up without snooze. On the bathroom mirror, in addition to his self-image reminder sheet, Ron has the list of new beliefs that he has decided to bring into his life. Ron+ has told him to say these beliefs out loud during his shower. Shower time is quite important to condition the mind as one tends to be quite relaxed, making the mind more open to suggestion. Saying new beliefs as auto-suggestions in the morning helps fix them in one's psychology. Ron has also started giving a better breakfast to his body.

The car pool is streamlined. Since there were only three guys and with one deciding to interrupt the usual pattern and replace it with more constructive one, there is not much the other two can do. Ron, for the first time, decides to discuss the book that he has been reading and how he realizes from reading it, that instead of focusing on discussing things beyond his control, he should try to focus on what he can improve within himself.

At office, Ron walks into the pantry, makes green tea and as expected, there is huge resistance from the peers, asking how come he could leave coffee, especially since he loved it so much. He takes this opportunity to announce to his colleagues that he wants to cut down on coffee and would like to solicit their support to do that. He requests them to remind him how great a degree of self-control he is already exhibiting by being able to quit it so far, each time he says he wants to have coffee. He asks them for their support as he should not break his resolve before the targeted fifteen days.

The peer group agrees. This strategy works as people feel responsible when they are assigned the responsibility.

Ron's way of working is also increasingly streamlined, as he tries to remain focused at work. Ron gets back home, runs, dines and gets ready for the session.

"Ron, the third element within Individuality is Charisma. In simplest terms, it is how the world sees you. Let's talk about it."

Principle 1: Charisma is the most powerful tool of persuasion and influence

"To emphasize its importance, I can tell you this – If there was just one skill you could master out of all the tools of persuasion and influence, it would be Charisma."

"Most times, people do not get what they want because they keep dreaming about things without taking action. They aspire for things without being willing to pay the price for them. People expect to get exceptional opportunities without making themselves exceptional. What they do not realize is that if they can become exceptional, those opportunities will naturally come their way. Their fundamental philosophy in life has been 'have-be', that is, they always had a 'having-before-becoming' mentality. What they do not realize is that life doesn't work like that. Life tends to work on 'be-have' principle, that is, 'becoming-before-having'. Be exceptional first and then attract the exceptional things naturally. Like the saying goes, 'How do you paint a perfect picture? Be perfect first and then paint normally!'"

> + ***"People expect to get exceptional opportunities without really making themselves exceptional."***

"Ron, as we discussed couple of days ago, people generally tend to like two kinds of people:

1. People who are related to them in some way or people who share similar interests – so they feel 'comfortable or at home' in their company
2. People who they aspire to be like, who inspire them and they view them as role models – so they feel 'awed' in their company"

"Charisma is more about the latter where you become someone who inspires other people to see the best within themselves. All great leaders such as Abraham Lincoln, Mahatma Gandhi and Martin Luther King are cited as examples for charismatic role models even today."

"If you ask me to point to the single most key ability of charismatic people, it would be their ability to develop quick rapport with others. To put it in simplest terms, rapport can be defined as 'understanding + trust'. When you are able to establish rapport with someone, you reach a stage where they feel fully understood and they place their trust in you. True rapport, comes from a place of absolute authenticity. You might think you can fake it, but you cannot. Maybe you can for a short time, but not for long. There is a sixth sense in humans that makes us sense the authenticity in others. We might not always be able to pinpoint it or express it in words, but deep down, we 'know'. Deep down there, is where rapport is built."

"To be authentically charismatic, it is important to feel 'congruent' within. 'Congruence' is a language that we might not understand consciously, but are looking for in our subconscious mind at all times. True congruence between our verbal and non-verbal language comes from full alignment with what we stand for, the ideas we believe in and why we do what we do. It is not easy to get to this place as it requires one to progress along areas of 'Self-image' and 'Beliefs', that we have already covered and along areas such as 'Passion' and 'Vision and Goals' that we will cover in the coming days."

Principle 2: Charisma is the sum total of multiple items, all of which can be worked upon

"Authenticity is a key component in charisma. But, it will take a while to get there. As you become aware of these principles, start working on them. With time, you will experience more alignment within and feel more congruent on what you want from your life and what direction you want to give it."

"In addition to this, we live in a world with set norms and expectations, both around personal and professional lives. Especially now that the world is becoming more interconnected, it is crucial to practise these norms so they come naturally to us. From this perspective, Charisma is really the sum total of a lot of aspects, both internal and external, all of which can be worked upon. I am covering the main aspects:

- **Dressing style**
    - Dress elegant
        - Research indicates that our clothes can account for ~95% of our first impression on others. Remember that the first impressions are almost always visual
    - Shop for quality, and not quantity
        - In addition to lasting longer, high-quality stuff makes one feel more comfortable and better about oneself and people around will be able to see your higher quality standards
- **Communication**
    - Become passionately interested in other people
        - With this one skill, you can win some real friends and strong business associates
    - Ask and remember names
        - Names are magical words to people and they instantly tend to like people who remember their names
    - Be respectful and considerate at all times
        - Irrespective of how people are to you, choose to be respectful and considerate at all times
        - Your behavior shows your standards, not the standards of people you are talking to
    - Develop listening skills
        - People appreciate being listened to. You can create strong rapport with people if you can just hear them out patiently
    - Refine your non-verbal communication
        - It is widely established that words communicate only 7% of our message with remaining 38% coming from our intonation and 55% coming from body language

- **Mannerisms**
    - Increase awareness
        - Refined etiquette works way better than a crude style in establishing rapport, especially with increasing globalization where it is critical to be aware and sensitive of cultural nuances
    - Develop a genuine smile
        - Smile is one of the most powerful expressions and a genuine one can light up a room
    - Be punctual
        - In both personal and professional lives, a super effective way to sincerely compliment others is to show them that you respect their time
- **Attitude**
    - Develop an optimistic attitude
        - Choosing to look at positive side of things and expecting favorable outcomes, not only makes other people want to spend time with you, but also reduces your stress levels in general
- **Professionalism**
    - Do more than you get paid for
        - The simplest way to invest in your career is to deliver more than you get paid for
        - Just this one thing will ensure that you learn more and gain credibility with more people
    - Under-promise over-deliver
        - Be it personal or professional context, people get delighted when they receive more than they expect

"If there is one overarching philosophy that you can keep in mind at all times so far as charisma is concerned, it would be this: You are a brand! Each time people think or hear about you, they visualize certain pictures and those pictures then evoke certain feelings within them."

> ***"If there is one overarching philosophy that you can keep in your mind at all times so far as charisma is concerned, it would be this: You are a brand!"***

"Starting to improve one's charisma is an exciting and rewarding journey in itself. The toughest part is starting, but if you can do that, you build momentum and don't want to stop! Remember Rumi's advice, 'If you feel irritated by every rub, how will you be polished?'"

"Also, remember that working on external elements alone seldom works. Even if it seems to work initially, the results will not last. For a real transformation to take place, both inside and outside need to go to the next level. Start from the internal, and then the external, and then, they reinforce each other!"

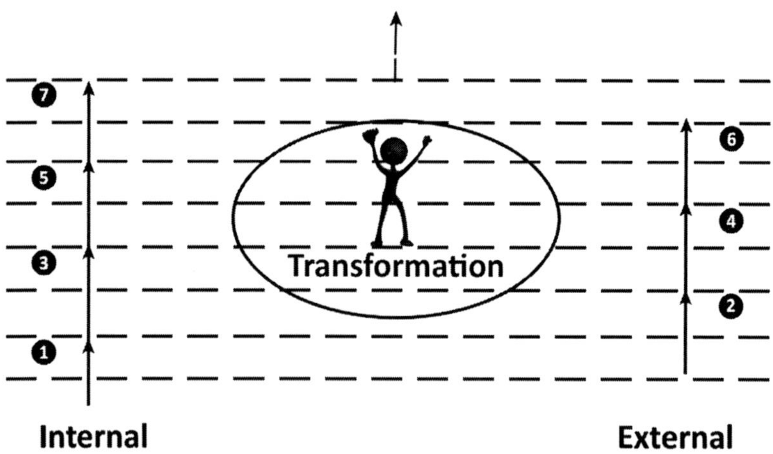

Figure 25: The transformation process: Reinforcement between internal and external

Principle 3: Extraordinary is a journey, not a destination

"The third principle in Charisma highlights how it is a long journey and that there is no end to how much one can improve. On your way, as you keep improving, you will naturally inspire others to take you as a role model. This can be one of the ways in which you contribute and share your learnings with others by making things simpler for them with your experience."

"That's interesting! What do you suggest I do?"

"Look at your life and really make it a point to become extraordinary. Look at everything in your life and ask yourself, 'What would be an ordinary response to this situation?'. This is easy. These are the responses that the untrained mind throws by default. Now, decide to do something that is slightly better than that response. Even a one percent improvement in everything you do, can give you a massive leap over time. Remember that even at ninety nine degree Celsius, water is still water. It is just that one last degree that transforms water into steam, strong enough to pull engines."

> *"Even at ninety nine degree Celsius, water is still water. It is just that one last degree that transforms water into steam, strong enough to pull engines."*

"I can give you three of my personal favorites among the small changes that made a big difference to my life:

1. At work, I make sure to check the document, presentation or email one last time before sharing it with others. Try this and trust me, you will almost always find at least one thing to be fixed!
2. At outings, I tip slightly more than average that leaves people delighted. It brings two benefits (i) they remember you next time you visit (ii) the extra tip will not make you poor, but rather, the increased positivity you create in the universe through the delight, will come back to you!
3. I carry books in my smartphone and tablet and read during 'waiting' times, that is, idle time when I am waiting for something or someone or time during travel e.g. in a taxi, metro etc. Over time,

I end up reading many books without even having to budget time for them!"

"This is just a start. You can come up with more of these small changes that are applicable to your specific context. Ron, focus on building the lifestyle of a successful person. Develop finer tastes, choose a calm and graceful disposition, refine your communication and cultivate a mindset of abundance. It is not enough to be yourself. You need to be your best self. As I already said, there is no end to this process. The best among us are not really more gifted than others. They just take more pains to stand their course even when they don't feel like it. The habit of giving in when you don't feel like it kills the possibility of extraordinary achievement."

> ***"Focus on building the lifestyle of a successful person. Develop finer tastes, choose a calm and graceful disposition, refine your communication and cultivate a mindset of abundance."***

"Ron, do you know how a genius is created?"

"Umm not really, tell me!"

"You start by learning the rules. You are diligent in practising them over and over for years. Once the rules are fully internalized, you start to break them. This is when your individuality starts to surface and you start to do things your own way. This is when you enhance the craft by producing 'originals'. As Miles Davis, Jr. said, 'Sometimes you have to play for a long time to be able to play like yourself'. The most key component here is discipline. We will talk about how one can introduce more discipline in one's life in the coming days."

Principle 4: Having a focus wider than your own self is a key element for charisma

"I think I understood the previous principles. What is this one about?"

"This one is about the next level. Let me explain! You can raise your charisma significantly if you work on the principles discussed earlier. But, you will still hit a ceiling. This is the journey to go from successful to significant. You can be successful with all these, but to be really significant, you need to focus outside yourself on something bigger than yourself. This is what I was referring to when I said you can start to teach others your learnings on the way, as early as you think you are ready for it. Remember, people do not follow other people, they follow causes. Leadership comes from envisioning something that doesn't yet exist and then fearlessly heading towards it taking along others who wish to go there too."

> ***"You can be successful with all these, but to be really significant, you need to have the focus outside yourself on something bigger than yourself."***

"Some kind of spiritual growth gets unlocked when you move beyond yourself to others. Try this for yourself. From where you are right now in life, start adding a few activities that impact more lives than your own and your immediate family and see the magic unfold! Your energy and resources will expand in the proportion of your span of consideration, that is, how many people you really care about. Here, people typically think that they will share once they have it, which is in contradiction to the law of intention that we talked about earlier. The more you keep 'wanting' before 'giving', the more you remain in the 'wanting' state. The moment you move into the 'giving' state, with whatever you can, you begin to attract a future for yourself where you continue to 'give' more. You are given more so you can give more. It might sound like I am talking about miracles here, but miracles happen only for people who believe that they happen. As Saint Augustine said, 'Miracles do not happen in contradiction to nature, but only in contradiction to that which is known to us of nature'. As Albert Einstein said, 'There are only two ways to live your life. One is as though nothing is a miracle. The other is as though everything is a miracle'. Both refer to the power of belief that we discussed yesterday."

"Ron, start to really believe that you are charismatic. Do the exercises and see how everything feeds into everything else to unleash an evolved version of yourself. Let's get to some exercises around building Charisma."

Exercise 1: Baseline your charisma: Do a current assessment of your charisma level

"The overall idea is to:

i. Assess your current self and establish the baseline
ii. Define your target aspiration
iii. Identify gaps
iv. Define steps to close them"

"Let's begin with your current assessment. I want you to rate yourself on a scale of 1-10 along each of the defined aspects. And please, do it sincerely! A lot of people do not take these exercises seriously. Remember what Peter Drucker said, 'What gets measured gets done!'"

Ron takes a while to think through and comes up with a scorecard for himself.

Table 4: Ron's current charisma level

Aspect	Current score
Dressing	7
Communication	7
Mannerisms	7
Attitude	5
Professionalism	6

Exercise 2: Design the leap to next level: Define the target charisma level

Ron takes a while and decides to target a score of 9 in each of the areas.

Table 5: Ron's target charisma level

Aspect	Current score	Target score
Dressing	7	9
Communication	7	9
Mannerisms	7	9
Attitude	5	9
Professionalism	6	9

"Okay, Ron. Now that you have the target scores, the next step is to design tasks on how you will raise your charisma level in each aspect. The tasks are fairly standard and the scores go higher based on how well you are able to do these tasks. It is not necessarily about adding many more new tasks."

They take some time to work together and come up with the list.

- **Dressing style**
    - Dress elegant
        - No matter what occasion, formal or informal, ensure that you dress elegant; overdressed is fine, under is not
    - Shop for quality, not quantity
        - Whatever quality you buy currently, go a notch higher now, even if it means you buy lesser quantity
- **Communication**
    - Become passionately interested in other people
        - People like to talk about themselves, ask them questions on what they like and not like (don't go overboard asking personal questions when you do not yet share that level of comfort with them!)
    - Ask and remember names

- There are a host of popular techniques that can help you remember names of people when you meet them, research these techniques, practise a few and adopt the ones that work best for you

- Be respectful and considerate at all times

  - Be friendly and caring to everyone you talk to all the time and use more of "please", "thank you" and "sorry" in your language; even if it is family members, try using these words and see how your life changes

- Develop listening skills

  - Strive to be a world-class listener; do not finish other peoples' sentences, no matter what!

- Refine your non-verbal communication

  - Train yourself to be consciously aware of your voice and body language at all times until it becomes natural for them to be consistent with your words

✦ **Mannerisms**

- Increase awareness

  - Become aware of and be sensitive to cultural differences

  - Refine your current mannerisms that may not show you in a very positive light

- Develop a genuine smile

  - Work on developing a genuine smile that reflects your authenticity

- Be punctual

  - Respect your and other peoples' time by always keeping your time commitments

✦ **Attitude**

- Be authentic

        - Be honest and frank; it is possible to be honest and frank with others while being emotionally sensitive and empathetic towards them

    - Develop an optimistic attitude

        - Once you alter your beliefs to more empowering ones, your attitude will automatically start being more positive

- **Professionalism**
    - Do more than you get paid for

        - Make it a habit to do what is expected and then do something more than that

    - Under-promise over-deliver

        - Make it a point to delight people who come in contact with you

Exercise 3: Take the leap to next level

"I leave it to you to decide how you want to do this exercise. You don't have to do it right away. Take your time to write down the steps it will take you to close the gap between your current and target scores. Start with the one-time activities you want to do and attach timelines to them. Once the plan is ready, put it at a place you can see it every day; bathroom mirror is always a good candidate! Some of the activities can be done quickly, while some others may take longer. Once you have a clear plan with timelines placed where it is visible, it is easy to monitor your progress."

Exercise 4: Once this iteration becomes natural, start all over again

"As you do this exercise, you will start to hit positive momentum. You will start liking the feeling of making progress. As you go further, another observation you will make is that as you evolve to a more charismatic person at a score of 9, from that position, when you rate yourself, you will again give yourself a 6 or 7 on all or some of the items. Your horizon would have expanded and you would have seen more possibilities. That observation will verify the assertion that becoming extraordinary is a journey. Once you reach your target state, you will realize there is more distance to cover. Repeat the exercises once you reach your defined current target state and redefine a new target!"

7. WHAT MAKES YOU COME ALIVE? (PASSION, DAY 5)

"Don't ask what the world needs, ask what makes you come alive and go do that, because what the world needs is people who have come alive." ~ Howard Thurman

The morning ritual and car pool seem fixed. Ron+ has indicated to Ron that once his new morning ritual becomes firm in three to four weeks, Ron must start waking up forty-five minutes earlier to move his run from evening to morning as exercising in the morning kick-starts the metabolism and energizes one for the rest of the day.

Work seems more positive than usual, understandably as it is Friday. It is strange how people understand that their moods are better on days they have something to look forward to, for instance, Fridays or the last few days in office before vacation. However, they still don't consciously design more of those elements into their lives and continue to suffer boredom.

This is day 5 of the ten days that Ron+ will stay with Ron. Ron already appreciates the wisdom of Ron+ in all life areas. Ron is happy that he is growing every day but is bit anxious at the same time as he realizes that knowledge by itself is not power. It becomes power only once it is applied correctly and consistently.

Knowledge by itself is not power. It becomes power only once it is applied correctly and consistently.

"Ron, let's talk about the first element within Inspiration. I call it 'Passion'; some others might call it 'Purpose' or 'Calling'. This is a sensitive topic among people for two reasons:

1. There is a widespread belief that people who found their passions are living ideal lives; I have already shared my views on how this might not be true
2. It is estimated that around 95% people do not know what they are passionate about and hence feel disappointed with discussions around this topic

My views on this topic are a bit strong. I really feel that some people use lack of a clear passion as a mechanism to rationalize and continue living within their comfort zones. Let's get into the details so you will understand my view better."

Principle 1: It is normal to not have a single passion in one's life

"Most people are like zombies, working in jobs week-in week-out. They are not fully happy but then not so unhappy either, that they go ahead and make any change. This in-between zone is commonly known as the 'comfort zone', and as we already discussed, is exactly where nothing of extraordinary significance is ever created! I can safely conclude that this is where you are too. Do you agree?"

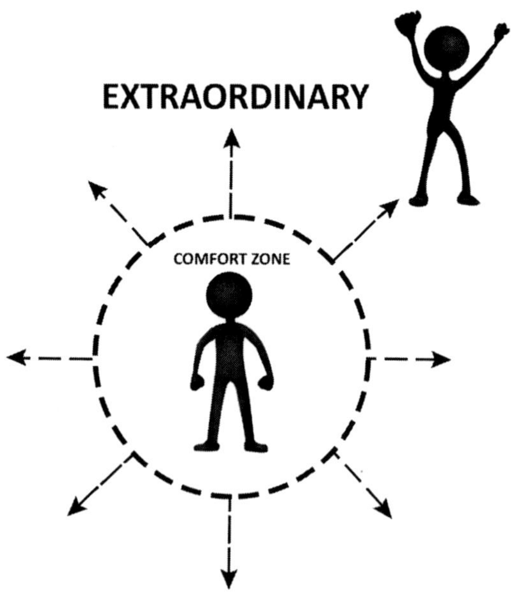

Figure 26: Comfort zone versus extraordinary

"Yes, pretty much!"

"Inspiration comes from being 'in spirit'. It is that magical feeling where you experience being 'in the zone'. Time does not exist, you do not exist, and you are completely unaware of your surroundings."

"Hmm… Can you share your views on the various means in which a person can get inspired?"

"In my experience, inspiration can come through one or more of the three means:

1. ***An art form*** – You might come across some form of art that really interests you. You start experimenting with it and realize that you can 'hit your zone' doing it
2. ***A role model*** – You come across a person who is either alive now or was in the past, and feel energized with their life stories and actions. It can be the vision set up by this person that fills you up with excitement. As Steve Jobs said, 'Let's make a dent in the universe'. These are inspiring words!
3. ***A higher cause*** – Some cause involving a community, may click with you and makes you feel strongly about it"

"It is estimated that 95% people do not know their passions. In my view, the real number is lesser. There are more people who know what interests them, just that they keep ignoring these interests so that their little worlds, that is, the comfort zones, are not disturbed. Taking concrete steps and moving in the direction of their dreams will require them to put in serious effort to do something new which would be a stretch from their regular lives."

> ***"There are more people who know what interests them, just that they keep ignoring these interests so that their little worlds, that is, comfort zones, are not disturbed."***

Principle 2: An interest becomes a passion not before you fight for it

"When you are passionate about something, you feel a fire within you. It's like finding something you can die for. It's like finding a cause that you can dedicate the rest of your life for. As Martin Luther King said, 'If you haven't found something worth dying for, you aren't fit to be living.' And the key thing really is this: When this fire first reveals itself to you, it reveals itself as a small spark. Some claim this is God's plan to test if you are capable of taking the idea and running with it. In my experience, these sparks are being revealed to people all the time. It's just that we are too busy to pay attention to the spark and even when we do, we let it die out, instead of protecting and feeding it until it grows into a magnificent flame for others to see and experience."

> ***"We are too busy to pay attention to the spark and even when we do, we let it die out, instead of protecting and feeding it until it grows into a magnificent flame for others to see and experience."***

"I strongly feel that it is not about the topic, but about people, who need to develop stronger mental muscles to fight for their sparks!"

"I understand! Do you have any suggestions around this?"

"It is possible to let everyone you meet, know that there's one thing about you that is not up for discussion: You are going to achieve your dreams no matter what others say about it. There is no room for compromise. Be absolutely certain in your mind and act as if what you desire has already happened."

> ***"It is possible to let everyone you meet, know that there's one thing about you that is not up for discussion: You are going to achieve your dreams no matter what others say about it."***

"One of the fundamental truths in life is that people, who get most approval from others, tend to care less about it. They have followed their heart and are independent of what others say about them. If they really listened to people around them, they may have stopped pursuing their passions long ago."

"Sure, I completely understand!"

Principle 3: Do not wait for life to give you your passions, bring your own passion to life

"Most people complain that they do not know their passions. I agree that there are people who do not know them. But if you look closely, you will find they do not even put in any efforts for this. They continue in their 9 to 5 jobs with their limiting beliefs. Any new idea is rejected. Given the understanding we have on self-image now, deep down, most people have conflicting desires and do not really see themselves worthy of big successes."

"In most cases, a passion doesn't appear automatically. A good way to start is to bring passion to everything you do. Making a goal out of finding your passion and chasing it directly, might only lead to anxiety and disappointment. Inspiration is a pure feeling. It is independent of the task and comes from the impact one creates. Do not always look outside to find inspiration. Bring inspiration to all that you do."

> +
> ***"Bring passion to everything you do. Making a goal out of finding your passion and chasing it directly, might only lead to anxiety and disappointment."***

"As I said couple of days ago, instead of complaining about the lack of passion, if everyone just becomes passionate about becoming their pluses, that is, better versions of themselves, the world will begin to transform. Think about this. If everyone was their best self, many of the problems we face in the world will immediately go away.

- If everyone was more engaged and mindful at their job, there would be less rework and mistakes, enhancing overall productivity
- If everyone felt good about themselves, they would complement others freely and initiate a network effort of appreciation, where positivity continues to expand as every person shares it with more people

- ✦ If everyone felt loved, they would share love with others and create thriving and fulfilling relationships
- ✦ And so on…"

"So Ron+, what do you recommend as a general approach?"

"Train yourself to show enthusiasm in all that you do. Being a positive feeling, enthusiasm has a high energy frequency and resonates closer to the creative power of the universe. In fact, the word enthusiasm comes from ancient Greek – 'en and theos' – meaning God. Another related word, 'enthousiazein' means 'to be possessed by God'. Since enthusiasm is a contagious feeling, the more you show it, the more people you attract to support you in all that you are trying to do."

"It is possible to bring your own enthusiasm. Having clarity on where you are headed in life, being content, and being fine with how you spend your time everyday are good ways to enable oneself to have higher enthusiasm overall."

"Let's do some exercises to assess and build on your passion levels."

Exercise 1: Baseline your passion: How much passion do you bring to each of your life areas?

"Ron, this is the first time you are doing this exercise. Let's begin with baselining your passion levels. Are you someone who is naturally more excited about life? Or are you dragging yourself along every day? On all life areas, score yourself 1-10 on the passion you think you bring to each of the areas. It will be great if you can also capture some points in the rationale or comments column."

Ron takes some time to fill out the table.

Table 6: Ron's current passion level

Life area	Your current score (1: Lowest, 10: Highest)	Rationale / Comments
Physical (Health)	6	Lack of time or that is how I have liked to think about it so far
Intellectual (Work)	7	I started quite high, but with time, since I feel I do not make as much impact as I would like to, this is going down
Social (Relationships)	6	Although my relationships are fine in general, lack of an intimate relationship makes me mark this low
Financial (Money)	8	I am fairly fine with this area, although there is significant opportunity to grow this further
Spiritual (Soul)	7	I have been feeling low over past few months, although I have enjoyed a decent level of alignment or congruence so far in my life

"Okay, fair enough! Let's look at how we can design where you want to go."

Exercise 2: Design the leap to next level: Think about how much passion you ideally want to bring to each of your life areas

"Ron, please indicate your target score for each of the areas. How much would you ideally like to score? Also, add comments on how you would know if that has happened."

Ron fills out his target table. He chooses a 9 for each of the target scores.

Table 7: Ron's target passion level

Life area	Target score	How would you know that has happened?
Physical (Health)	9	I will experience a higher energy level and vitality consistently I will be able to run at least a half-marathon regularly
Intellectual (Work)	9	I will experience more autonomy in decision-making at my work I will have more opportunity to express my creativity at work
Social (Relationships)	9	I will have a loving and passionate intimate relationship I will experience enriched relationships with my family, friends, colleagues and acquaintances
Financial (Money)	9	I will be able to increase my income and investment potential by at least 50% I will make progress in building additional revenue streams especially passive ones, that is, where I make money without my direct involvement
Spiritual (Soul)	9	I will be able to feel more calmness and stillness inside me I will be able to find that sense of absolute certainty inside me that everything happens for my greater good

Exercise 3: Take the leap

"Since we have already conducted this exercise couple of times, I will leave this to you. Make a list of activities and tasks that you need to do to achieve these scores. Organize them into a roadmap with timelines as you did for

Charisma. As you put activities against timelines, it will become easy to track progress."

"Find out areas where you are holding yourself back the most and dig deeper to understand the root causes. These are the areas where, if you make progress, you will be able to provide a strong impetus to all other areas. In your case, it could be physical, that is, your health. Since you have never focused on this area before, you do not know how it will be to feel more energetic than you do now. It might enable you to use that extra energy to progress in other areas. It can be the same with relationships. Once you feel comfortable, loved and secure in your relationships, your motivation to progress in other areas might increase significantly."

Exercise 4: Potential areas of passion: List the areas you are interested in

"Once you become someone who brings more passion to everything that you do, you will be closer to identifying those few topics that ignite you with total enthusiasm. Let me introduce to you two powerful exercises that can help you here:

1. Sit in a comfortable and quiet place. Relax your mind and ask yourself, 'If I was to be given my financial independence today, that is, I do not have to work for money anymore, what is it that I would like to do all day?' Visualize yourself living that life. See what your home would look like. See who you will have around you. See what you see yourself doing. Hear what you will be hearing. Feel what you will feel then. In most instances, the activities that you see yourself doing, will give you an indication of the activities or topics you are enthusiastic about
2. Spend time increasing your awareness about the world of unconventional careers, and see what others are doing with their lives. Observe them with an open mind without letting your mind jump in to tell you how it would not work in your case. Our minds are really good at this! I am not telling you to see what others are doing so that you can imitate them. I want you to become more aware. See if there is anything that resonates with you."

"Ron, do you have a vision? Is there something that you absolutely want to do in this life?"

"Well, as I told you earlier, I have been struggling to find the answers to my questions for years now. If I can find the answers, I would like to share them with as many people as I can, so that they do not have to struggle as much."

"Fantastic, that is quite a noble thought. Let me caution you beforehand. When you start, it is possible that you face resistance from people around you. The key is to keep at it until you succeed. As Arthur Schopenhaur said, 'All truths go through three steps:

1. It is ridiculed
2. It is violently opposed
3. It is accepted as self-evident'"

"As Mahatma Gandhi said, 'First they ignore you, then they laugh at you, then they fight you, then you win'. Over the coming days, we will cover the topic of 'Mind Control' that is about building a stronger mental muscle to help you hang in there even when the going gets tough. Of course, if you continue to persist, you will get there eventually!"

"Thanks Ron+ for your encouragement. I was thinking about this just a few days ago. Even if I have a vague idea on wanting to do something different, I do not even have five people around me who believe that I can do it. How under such circumstances, can I even imagine achieving it?"

"I understand. But, you are not the only one! Most people do not have these five people around them. It is not easy but, it is not impossible either, to build a network of positive people around you. If you really want to realize your goal, you will find people who will encourage you no matter what. For most self-help and personal development concepts to work, it is important to have an environment that enables you. Or else, you will be sucked back into our LAU!"

"What's LAU?"

"Not something standard! I just made it up – Life-As-Usual!"

They both laugh. "Ron, let's call it a day now. We will discuss 'Mind Control' in detail in the coming days."

8. WHAT IS YOUR VISION? (GOALS, DAY 6)

"When a man does not know what harbor he is making for, no wind is the right wind" ~ Seneca

This is the weekend. It is the right time to engage in something that is important and takes longer to discuss. Ron+ had already told Ron that he wanted to reserve first day of the weekend for a topic that is quite critical for anyone's success. One cannot define success without this being in place. This is the day to talk about visioning and goal setting. Without a vision or goals in place, how will one know if they are successful? In the race to 'have', people accumulate without knowing how much is really 'enough'. If there is no contentment, any amount will not be.

What needs to happen for you to call yourself 'successful'?

Ron finishes his morning rituals. He does a 30-minute run too! Ron+ comes in, his usual self, calm, serene, wise and content. While Ron is sipping green tea, he tells Ron+ how badly he misses coffee, and how a cup of coffee on a weekend morning will be just perfect.

Ron+ chuckles, "Ron, have a longer term perspective. You are on a journey that will transform your life. You will produce better results going forward in all life areas. Just indulge me. It is only fifteen days. You won't die! We are doing this so that the accomplishment increases your inner strength and convinces you that you can do this and tougher things in the time to come."

+ ***"You are on a journey that will transform your life. You will produce better results going forward in all life areas."***

"Sure, I understand! I can wait!"

"I will tell you a little about how some addictions work. Contrary to what you expect, you do not feel the worst on day one. You feel it around day three or four, after which you feel fine again. With coffee, you are exactly at that point. I totally empathize with you. Once you cross this, things will get better."

"Let's talk about core principles of the second element within the pillar of 'Inspiration'"

Principle 1: A compelling vision is the first step for all transformation (same as having 'be' goals)

"Ron, there is a saying 'A person who doesn't know where he is going, usually gets there'. In fact, a key requirement if you want to be extraordinarily average in your life is to not have a vision for yourself and take life as it comes."

"Goal setting is discussed in all kinds of personal and professional development training programs. But, the focus still tends to be on 'have' goals, that is, people are encouraged to write down what they want to have in next one, five or ten years. As examples: 'I want to have one million dollars in my bank' or 'I want to have a Ferrari'. Having 'have' goals is fine, I am not against them. But they are more linked to leading a comfortable life and that's all about it. You cannot expect fulfilment coming from 'have' goals."

"Fulfilment comes from 'be' goals, that is, who you want to be in one, five or ten years. As examples: 'I want to be an accomplished author' or 'I want to be a successful businessman'. Creating 'be' goals is like creating a vision for you. That is why I call this exercise as 'visioning'. A compelling vision is the first step for all transformation as it provides the required 'why'. As Friedrich Nietzsche said, 'He who has a why to live can bear almost any how'"

"Real happiness and contentment come only from becoming 'more' and not just 'having' more. We saw how the law of creation works. One cannot even 'have' before 'being'. Irrespective of whether you are convinced of the law or not, start from 'be' goals. Ensure that the vision you create is not easy but a stretched one. As Michelangelo said, 'The greatest danger for most of us lies not in setting our aim too high and falling short; but in setting our aim too low, and achieving our mark'"

> + ***"Real happiness and contentment in life can come only from becoming 'more' and not just 'having' more."***

"Once you have a compelling vision for yourself with concretely defined steps on how to get there, you will experience a new sense of freedom. Yes, it might sound counterintuitive, but it's true. You will not be too bothered with what your friends and colleagues are doing once you are excited to make your vision a reality. As Henry Ford said, 'Obstacles are those frightful things you see when you take your eyes off your goal'"

Principle 2: It is fine to make 'have' goals as they give a more tangible feel, however, they should never cloud the main 'be' goals

"I encourage you to make both kinds of goals. Start from the 'be' goals. How do you see yourself in the next one, five or ten years? Then move to 'have' goals. For your 'have' goals, you need to know why you want to 'have' them as it is not really the 'having' that makes you want it. There is a corresponding need that that thing would satisfy for you or some emotion that it allows you to experience."

"Both the 'be' and 'have' goals continue to evolve as you progress and achieve some of them. As you 'be' someone, you want to 'be' more, as you 'have' some things, you want to 'have' some others. That is the natural progress that human spirit thrives on."

> + ***"Both 'be' and 'have' goals continue to evolve as you progress and achieve some of them."***

Principle 3: Unwritten goals are better known as wishes; goals needs to be written down, specific and time-bound

"Ron+, it feels so weird to write down goals, do people usually do it?"

"Most people never write their goals down. Owing to this reluctance, they lose out on the big benefits that come about from having written down goals."

> + *"Something magical happens when you write your goals down."*

"Can you elaborate how that happens?"

"Sure, something magical happens when you write your goals down:

- By writing them down, you make your goals come alive, that is, you bring them into existence and they are not the same as other thoughts that you think every day. It is estimated that we think 60,000 thoughts every day with 95% of them being same as those from the previous day!
- The process of writing them down engages our motor mechanism, that is, our physical body, thereby registering them more deeply within our nervous systems
- As we discussed within 'Beliefs', our mind, more so the subconscious mind, is a solution-seeking mechanism. Since our perception cannot take in all the sensory inputs we receive, it filters information to bring only limited content within our perception. Once we assign clear goals, the mind starts to filter in information relevant to them. You would have observed this for yourself. When you consider buying something, say some model of a car, you start seeing it everywhere, on billboards that you passed by many times before but never noticed them until now. Once you write your goals down, it is possible to put them in an accessible place, for example, the bathroom mirror where you can see them every day. Seeing them in the morning helps you start your day directing your mind to get into your focus all those things that will take you closer to your goals

- Written down goals are easier to share with others. There are multiple views on whether one should share their goals with others or not. Some schools of thought recommend not sharing them with anyone and keeping them a total secret as these are your goals, and, instead of dissipating your energy on telling them to others, you should channelize energy towards the actual attainment of these goals. Another school of thought says that one should declare their goals openly to the universe. This has clear positives in terms of attracting more like-minded people into your life and driving you to work towards them, as you have increased accountability since you told so many people that you were going to do it.

  I personally like the latter approach more. When you disclose your goals to another person, you can have only three reactions:

  1. The other person gets excited for you and connects you with some resources and people who are into similar fields so you can directly benefit from their experience
  2. The other person is indifferent and doesn't react much, but by just saying them aloud one more time, you reinforce your goals to yourself
  3. The other person tries to put you down and claims that you will never be able to achieve your goals. I understand that with this reaction, there is a possibility that you get discouraged, but that is for people who are not aware of these principles. In your case, these are the people who will actually help you train your mental muscle and mind control and end up working in your favor. We will talk more about this tomorrow on how you can do this

- Lastly, as written down goals are tangible 'things', they are easy to keep handy. They can serve as your counsel towards maintaining a long-term perspective in life. This helps people make better decisions in the short-term, while bringing in excitement in life with the mundane tasks seeming more meaningful. Instead of seeing your job as something that keeps you stuck, you view it as something that pays your bills and allows you to gradually move closer to your larger goals

> **"Written down goals are easy to keep handy and can serve as your counsel towards maintaining a long-term perspective in life."**

Principle 4: Progress towards your goals daily and have fun on the way

"On the way to achieving your goals, ensure that you build two aspects:

1. ***Take at least one small step towards your goal everyday*** – It will maintain the momentum while constantly signaling to your subconscious that you are determined to achieve your goal and are disciplined about it. If you have more than one goal, it might not be possible to pursue all of them daily. Ensure that you take a small step on each, once a week
2. ***Reward yourself on attainment of both small and big milestones*** – It is common knowledge in human motivation that whatever gets rewarded gets reinforced. This is a key aspect in ensuring that the momentum stays. Reward yourself when you achieve milestones on the way to your goals. For instance, take a nice evening out with your friends, or buy something you always wanted to have, or any other thing that works for you when you achieve a milestone"

"Okay, enough of theory! Let's do some exercises."

Exercise 1: Create a long-term vision for yourself, that is, what do you want to 'be' when you are 40 / 50 / 60 along each of the five life areas

"Ron, this is an important exercise. Ensure that you put enough seriousness into it. It will give you the direction you are headed in life. This can be done alone or with a group of trusted people. Use a whiteboard if it is easily accessible. If not, do it on paper. Brainstorm individually or collectively on how you would want to 'be' when you are 40, 50 or 60 years old. How do you want other people to know you? How do you want to feel? Do this for each of your life areas. This is your long-term vision. It will be tough to do this exercise without focusing on what you want to 'have'. But, please indulge me. Do it for the 'be' first and then you will get a chance to go for the 'have' goals."

"Okay, as you say, Ron+!"

Ron comes up with the following long-term vision.

Table 8: Long-term vision – 'Be' goals

Life area	'Be' goal
Physical (Health)	Be full of energy all the time
Intellectual (Work)	Be a renowned expert with strong technical expertise in my area of work
Social (Relationships)	Be loved by my family and everyone I associate with
Financial (Money)	Be financially independent i.e. I do not need to work for money anymore. I can provide for my family easily, and feel secure with the assets I have built over all these years
Spiritual (Soul)	Be content and fulfilled with the life I have lived by making a positive impact to lives of others around me

"Okay. Now that you have done the 'be' exercise, I want you to do the 'have' exercise. You can extend the same table."

Ron includes the 'have' goals as well.

Table 9: Long-term vision – 'Be' and 'Have' goals

Life area	'Be' goal	'Have' goal
Physical (Health)	Be full of energy all the time	Have a healthy and fit body
Intellectual (Work)	Be a renowned expert with strong technical expertise in my area of work	Have written a couple of books or papers in my area of expertise Have board positions in a few companies in the area Have ownership in a few startups in the area
Social (Relationships)	Be loved from my family and everyone I associate with	Have a large family (sons, daughters, grandchildren) together or close by Have a close group of like-minded associates
Financial (Money)	Be financially independent i.e. I do not need to work for money anymore. I can provide for my family easily, and feel secure with the assets I have built over all these years	Have couple of properties across the world Have a nice house where I live with my family Have sufficient amount of liquid assets
Spiritual (Soul)	Be content and fulfilled with the life I have lived by making a positive impact to lives of others around me	*Guess gets covered in the 'be' goal*

"Okay, Ron. How do you feel when you look at this table?"

"I feel I am full of optimism and excited about the good future I can have. When I look at this, I wonder why I get so anxious about my everyday life when it is going to unfold in such a positive way eventually!"

"Ron, the anxiety is there because you have not formalized your vision. Once you formalize the vision, you realize that all anxiety vanishes. Now that we have the 'long-term vision', let's move to the next step."

Exercise 2: Work backwards to create a vision for yourself over next five years along each life area

"Working backwards from your 'long-term vision', do the same thing over next five years and ensure you cover all life areas. For each area, envision how you want to be, followed by what you would like to have."

Ron follows the instructions and comes up with the table.

Table 10: Five-year vision – 'Be' and 'Have' goals

Life area	'Be' goal	'Have' goal
Physical (Health)	Be more energetic than I currently am Be able to run full marathons on a regular basis	Have a healthy and fit body
Intellectual (Work)	Starting to be recognized as an expert with strong technical expertise in my area of work	Have written at least one book in the area of my expertise Have ownership in at least one startup in my interest area
Social (Relationships)	Be fully balanced within myself so that I can be nicer to people around as I will be free from my own internal struggles Starting to be loved more from my family and everyone I associate with	Have found my soul-mate, someone who fully understands me and I want to build my life with Have a close group of like-minded associates
Financial (Money)	Be financially strong and on track to financial independence, that is, continue to progress on enhancing my earning potential	Have a nice house where I live with my family Have sufficient amount of liquid assets
Spiritual (Soul)	Be more content and peaceful with the way I live my life and with where it is headed	*Guess gets covered in the 'be' goal*

Exercise 3: Perform a gap assessment between your current and your envisioned self; develop a roadmap with milestones and timelines to bridge it

"Once you define your target state for next five years, assess yourself on each area and identify the gaps. Individually or collectively, as the case may be, pick activities that appeal to you and you wish to have in your life to help you close these gaps. Let's work together on your list and see what activities we can come up with."

They work together and come up with a list of activities for Ron that will help him bridge the gaps between his current and target defined states.

Table 11: Activities to bridge the five-year gap

Life area	Activities to bridge the gap
Physical (Health)	Start running for 30-60 minutes every morning Start going to the gym for fitness and strength training Start eating healthy
Intellectual (Work)	Start devoting dedicated time to activities that build my knowledge and network in the area of my interest Start getting involved in Venture Capital and Angel networks
Social (Relationships)	Find like-minded associates and spend more time with them Start to 'be' like the person I want to attract in my life
Financial (Money)	Focus on increasing my earning ability Start focusing on building long-term wealth
Spiritual (Soul)	Start to meditate and create time for stillness in otherwise busy life Focus on increasing intuition and listening to my inner guide

"Once the activities are identified, create a roadmap and timeline for them. Remember, doing this exercise with another person or other people, brings additional benefit of an increased sense of accountability that puts more pressure on you. That is a personal preference though. Feel free to choose between doing it alone or with others. The best arrangement here and in previous exercises where you have activities to be done with proper timelines, is to have at least one person, who can be your accountability partner. You can even split this program and have multiple accountability partners depending on the activities. To illustrate, you can have a personal trainer for your physical goals, a yoga teacher for your spiritual goals, and so on. You can have a Success/ Life/ Performance Coach as the partner in this overall program to whom you can report your progress on a regular basis and seek feedback. We will elaborate on structuring this in the days to come."

"Thanks Ron+! This day was helpful! I feel more in control now that I see my goals clearly written down. My mind is already starting to go into 'solution mode' instead of staying in 'problem mode'. It is telling me 'what needs to happen for me to get there' rather than 'why I cannot get there'"

"Sure Ron, you are most welcome! I am glad it is helping!"

On that note, they end first day of the weekend that can be called quite a transformational weekend for Ron.

9. HOW TO ASSIGN EMPOWERING MEANINGS? (MIND CONTROL, DAY 7)

"I don't wait for moods. You accomplish nothing if you do that. Your mind must know it has got to get down to work" ~ Pearl S. Buck

Second day of the weekend begins like the previous day. Ron was informed that this day would be devoted to a skill that can dramatically change anyone's life if mastered. This morning Ron also has his five-year vision with the 'have' goals pasted on the bathroom mirror.

"Ron, let's get into our discussion."

Principle 1: The ability to master our minds and assign empowering meanings is the most important tool in self-help and personal development

"In your pursuit towards your goals, you have to have a strong mental muscle. What I mean is that as events continue to happen, you need to be able to assign them positive meanings and take results as feedback instead of full and final failure. People, who fail and stop, become content with their failures. People who are absolutely committed to success carry on despite the number of disappointments they encounter. They do not stop until they absolutely obtain what they are looking for."

"Using the soccer analogy, I can say that all the time, you meet people who are complaining about how they are not even getting the ball to score. When you dig deeper, you realize that they left the playing field long back. They are sitting in the stands! Something in their life hit them so hard that they never got up. They sat down within! We know how soccer works. It is not possible to get the ball each time you want to score. Sometimes you just need to wait, but ensure that it is not a 'passive wait'. Rather, make it an 'active wait'."

> ***"People complain on how they are not even getting the ball to score. When you dig deeper, you realize they left the playing field long back."***

"In the game of life, you do not have full control on choosing to be the player who scores the most goals. You might not always get the ball, but you can definitely be the player who scores each time they get the ball. If you can do that or not will depend on what you do when you do not have the ball. Do you complain about not getting a chance or you continue to better your game? Remember this: The world will not remember you for all the times you fail. It will remember you for the one time that you do not. Mind control is all about developing that discipline and getting up each time you fall down."

> ***"The world will not remember you for all the times you fail. It will remember for the one time that you do not."***

"This sounds quite interesting! Can you tell me more about this?"

"It takes time to get ingrained fully, but will never get done unless you start. Remember, we started this discussion in our early days. Start intervening in that moment of 'I' when you get to know of something or something happens and you assign a meaning to it. You already assign meanings every minute of your life, just that you do it unconsciously. Going forward, you meanings need to be more deliberate and empowering."

"Your overall beliefs have a key role to play in this. You will not be able to assign meanings that are in contradiction to your beliefs. In this light, it should not come to you as a surprise when I tell you that one of the beliefs of highly successful people is that 'Everything happens for the good'. This belief ensures that the meaning assignment mechanism assigns positive meanings. As Stan Dale said, 'I've always been the opposite of a paranoid. I operate as if everyone is part of a plot to enhance my well-being'. Now, that's definitely a good attitude to adopt!"

"It is unfortunate that structured education systems do not teach people about how their minds function. Practising mind control is a fundamental skill to living life and whatever we focus on, makes us feel accordingly. Recall memories from your last most amazing vacation versus moments where you were really embarrassed and see how you instantly begin to feel in both cases. You will be able to appreciate the direct correlation between what we choose to focus on and how we feel."

> ***"Recall memories from your most amazing last vacation versus moments where you were really embarrassed and see how you instantly begin to feel in both cases."***

"Oh, so is that why there is a constant push for positive thinking?"

"Yes. The core philosophy behind all positive thinking is related to this. You are being asked to consciously focus on positive side of things. When you do that, you feel emotions that make you feel good, and then you decide how you will act based on those emotions."

"I am sure you have seen how on some days, you wake up feeling upbeat, and you automatically feel like being nice to everyone around. We have talked about these days earlier as well. On these days, don't you find it easier to focus better at work? These days are a clear testimony to the assertion that our 'Inner World' defines our 'Outer World'. With time-tested principles from the science of achievement, you can simply learn to put yourself in this state at your own discretion."

"I will give you the steps to show you how this works:

1. An event happens
2. We choose what side of the event we focus on i.e. positive or negative
3. We assign an empowering/ neutral/ disempowering meaning
4. We feel a corresponding emotion
5. In that moment we decide what we will do
6. We take action"

Ron wants to interrupt. "Hold on Ron, I know exactly what you want to say! You want to say that you never do steps 2, 3 and 5. Correct?"

"How did you know, Ron+?"

"That's what everyone says once this concept is presented to them. We are used to knowing that humans are creatures of emotion and not logic. Let me tell you something. We might be calling ourselves creatures of emotion but there is a consistent logic to how we feel the emotions."

> + ***"We might be calling ourselves creatures of emotion but there is a consistent logic to how we feel the emotions."***

"What do you mean, Ron+?"

"Let me explain with an example. Imagine there are two colleagues A and B. A comes across a great opportunity to further his career. To this, B has four potential response options.

1. B can be indifferent as it is A's life
2. B can encourage A out of his goodness
3. If B thinks logically, he can see this as a positive opportunity to further his own career and encourage A to take it up, knowing that as A becomes prosperous, A will create more opportunities for B as well
4. B discourages A, despite it being clear that it is a good opportunity for A"

"Where does option 4 come from? Since we are creatures of emotion, what sometimes gets triggered in such a situation is option 4. B gets jealous and discourages A from taking up the opportunity. B rationalizes by saying it can be too risky or might not work out for A and so it is not a good decision to take it up. On the inside however, B might know that he is not being fully honest. If you ask B why he reacted that way, he will tell you that we are creatures of emotion and when emotions take over, we cannot think logically."

"What I am saying here is that to feel any emotion, we need to focus on something. In this case, it happened unconsciously. B, in his unconscious/subconscious mind, very quickly ran all the assessment thinking how, if A takes this opportunity, he would get ahead of B. This is where the feeling of jealousy comes from. For untrained minds, this process is unconscious. Since we are so used to running these patterns every day, in real life, it comes across as:

1. An event happens
2. *(Unconscious)*
3. *(Unconscious)*
4. We feel a corresponding emotion
5. *(Unconscious)*
6. We take action"

"As you can see, by losing control on steps 2, 3 and 5, we lose control on deciding how to feel and choosing what to do accordingly. You will also appreciate how people who are stuck in negative patterns continue to remain there and continue to dislike their jobs or their relationships simply because they continue to focus on the negative aspects of each, and are unable to 'think differently' about them."

> ***"You can appreciate how people who are stuck in negative patterns continue to remain there and are unable to 'think differently' about their situation."***

"Sure, I get it now!"

"Ron, to become prosperous, you do not necessarily have to be a successful entrepreneur. You just have to believe in a potential successful entrepreneur. You will be able to identify them only once you are in the abundance mindset. Otherwise, you will continue to kill all potential chances of becoming prosperous by becoming jealous when you meet these people, as most others do, and continue to remain stuck where they are."

"Can you give me some examples on how this can be applied in our day-to-day lives?"

"Sure. A core idea in mind control is to increase the level of your consciousness, that is, do not let petty things bother you. Be aware that every person defines 'petty' differently. Even for the same person, the definition of 'petty' might change as they go along with life. One of the ways to test your success with mind control is to check on the level of things that bother you currently. It is like the difference between standing in the middle of a busy road where it is loud. You smell the pollution, there are too many people trying to cross the road, pushing you from side to side. When you stand there, everything will seem to bother you!"

"If on the other hand, you take a higher view, say you go on top of a tall building, how would you feel there? There is less noise. You have fresh air. No one pushes you around. You have a lovely view. The same holds for life. Look at yourself and assess the level of problems that bother you. You may have seen people getting angry at waiters for goofing up their orders. If you live a bit higher, you might not get agitated over these things. You might take this as an opportunity to grow yourself, that is, to test your patience level, or to test if you can eat the dish with little less salt. If you can, it might just be better for you to move onto that for the long-term. If there genuinely was a goof-up, others will realize their mistakes and appreciate you for your patience. So all in all, you leave everyone in a positive mood and maintain positivity in the universe, instead of shouting at the waiters, and spoiling your day from where you continue to spoil everyone else's day. Spoiling the day for others will have a ripple effect as they will pass it onto people they come in touch with. So in essence, you start something with your shouting and you do not even know how much negative energy it can create in the universe, and how its impact might come back to you."

"Wow! I never thought about this ripple effect of the negative energy that we create in ourselves and others. I need to be more careful going forward!"

"True. Now that you are conscious of this, try to leave everyone you meet in a better state than they were before they met with you."

+ ***"Always try to leave everyone you meet in a better state than they were before they met with you."***

"Ron+, I understand that I can use my mental muscle to control the way I feel. What else can I do with it?"

"Controlling your emotions is the biggest impact. It is strong enough to transform your life already. You can also start using your mental muscle for other things. For instance, when you are on a flight and feel sleepy, close your eyes and begin to sleep. Use your imagination to imagine that you are sleeping on your bed, feel the texture of your sheets, feel the softness of your pillow, and feel the temperature of your room. Just doing this will enable you to sleep better and you will wake up lot more refreshed than otherwise. The same approach can be applied in a situation where you are feeling cold. In your mind, bring forth the memories of a time where you felt hot. Replay them with the same intensity in your mind. You will be surprised that you are not feeling cold anymore. This can be applied when you are feeling hot and want to feel cooler, too. The same techniques of mind control can play a key role in managing stress as well."

"Can you please elaborate on this?"

"Ron, it is quite simple. Stress happens when we give something more importance than we should and we do it primarily because we get stuck in the moment and are not able to detach ourselves from it. Each time you face a problem and are fully absorbed in solving it, take a step back and think of what the impact of this problem would be in five years from now."

> ***"Each time you face a problem and are fully absorbed in solving it, take a step back and think of what the impact of this problem would be in five years from now."***

"Finding positives in life is an art. Even after severe traumas, some people experience positives. Surviving a trauma tends to increase peoples' inner strength and they are not scared of that anymore. Crisis situations provide a good test to check on ones' relationships. You get to separate your real friends from others. This is highly dependent on how you view the traumatic situation. If you assign a meaning saying God is punishing you, you will be disempowered. If you assign that God is making you stronger to prepare you for bigger and better opportunities, you will really come out stronger."

Principle 2: The power of choice, and we almost always have it, is the second most important tool in self-help and personal development

"We are making choices all the time. The key to achieving more in life lies in that moment of choice. That is the magical moment when we exercise our free will. You might have come across a lot of fatalistic people who claim there is no free will and everything is destined. Or they will claim that there is free will in low-impact choices such as what you will eat but not in high-impact choices such as what job you will get. From my experience, let me tell you this: The low-impact choices made consistently over years lead to high-impact outcomes."

> + ***"The low-impact choices made consistently over years lead to high-impact outcomes."***

"Freedom is not the absence of commitments, but rather the ability to choose and commit oneself to what is best for them. To eat more or less is a choice. To exercise or not is a choice. To smoke or not smoke is a choice. To make a relationship work or not is a choice. To give 100% commitment at your work or not is a choice. To mistreat others or not is a choice. In fact, choice is such a powerful indicator that you can look at the choices a person makes and guess where they are headed in life. Remember that all choices have causal consequences."

> + ***"You can look at the choices a person makes and guess where they are headed in life."***

"This is why I say it is important to have clear vision and goals, so that all our choices become consistent in a particular direction. The winds are random and are the same for everyone, but the sailor who knows where he is going can adjust his sail accordingly. Another way to look at it is, although the winds are same for everyone, you can see boats going in different directions because each sailor has their sail adjusted based on where they want to go. Where you will go is not a function of the winds, but really of how you set your sails."

> *"Where you will go is not a function of the winds, but really of how you set your sails."*

"Once you have the picture of your vision or goal clear in your mind, you will be able to ask yourself each time, 'What choice will take me closer to that and what choice will take me away?' and then choose accordingly."

"Ron, life is not what is happening to us, but what we 'think' is happening to us. Two boys from the same alcoholic father can have different destinies based on the meanings they assign to their birth in that family and the corresponding decisions they take. One who takes it as a 'punishment' will choose to suffer and become an alcoholic, inflicting the same pain on others around him. The other who chooses to take it as a 'reason', will elevate himself and become a volunteer, helping rehabilitation of other alcoholics and their families."

"In another case, parents who really wanted a boy, but have a girl instead, have two choices. One, they can say that God does not love them and in return, they will not accept the girl as they never wanted her. Or they can say, since they wanted a boy and God gave them a girl, maybe there is a higher meaning in this. Maybe she will do something that has never been done by a girl before, so let's do our best to raise her! Don't you think that the experiences of these three souls will be different based on what the parents decide to choose?"

Principle 3: Listening more to your intuition and less to others is critical for mind control

"Ron, you are not alone in this journey of life. There is a senior partner with you all the time. This holds true only if you acknowledge its presence. To have a strong mental muscle, it will be helpful if you have a strong spiritual muscle. Like every other muscle, the only way to strengthen it is to train it. In the pursuit of your vision and goals, there will be times when things will not seem to be going the way you expected them to and all visible doors will seem to be closed. In these times, you will be feeling low, and will need to rely on your spiritual muscle."

"The only way to strengthen a muscle is to train it."

"To make friends with the creative force, the first step is to focus on how you feel at any moment. There are hundreds of words that can describe how you feel. But broadly, there are just three: good, neutral or bad. Feeling good brings you closer to the creativity zone while feeling bad takes you away from it."

"We have touched upon this earlier. Let me elaborate. The creation process is really that simple, you need to:

1. Visualize the outcome with full vividness and intensity as if it were really happening to you
2. Feel the feelings you will feel if it were really happening
3. Show patience and receive it gracefully when you get it"

"As Dr. Wayne Dyer said, 'Prayer is when we talk to God, Intuition is when God talks to us'. Pray with your full force and then make space to receive the answers. We almost always get them, though sometimes not in the same shape or form as we expected them to come in."

"Try to focus on the source rather than the material things. As the anecdote goes, 'A man was washing his new car when his neighbor asked him, 'You got a new car?' He replied 'My brother gave it to me.' The neighbor said, 'I wish I had a car like that.' The man replied, 'I thought you were going to wish to have a brother like that' or maybe 'becoming a brother like that'"

"A very important element in achieving your goals will be 'making yourself independent of the opinion of others'. As I said earlier, it is rather unfortunate but true that we live in a negative society. You can find hundreds of people who will tell you how you will not be able to achieve your goals compared to the few who will genuinely encourage you. Typically, the people who will demotivate you will be the ones who were either too scared to try new things in their own lives or are afraid that you might succeed."

+ ***"A very important element in achieving your goals will be 'making yourself independent of the opinion of others'"***

"You meet two kinds of people. One kind will always give you specific and unsolicited advice on what you should be doing in various aspects of your life. I do not have anything against these people. They live in a world where others around them do the same to them and this is their way of expressing their love and consideration for you. The challenge is that since every person is a unique combination of 'self-image + beliefs', their advice is colored by their own life experiences and expectations. The other kind of people is the ones who believe in the power of listening to one's inner voice. No matter what problem you present to these people and no matter which of these people you present the problem to, they will always give you one advice 'Listen to yourself and go with what you hear!'"

"As Robert Frost wrote, 'Two roads diverged in a wood, and I took the one less traveled by, and that has made all the difference'. When I say become indifferent, I do not mean you stop caring about how you impact the people around you. What I am really suggesting here is this: If you really listen to your intuition and act accordingly, there will be some people around you who will not agree with you. By all means, respect their opinions. But you do not have to conform to them. Following your intuition might not be the sole formula to become extraordinary, but listening to others and conforming each time is definitely the sole formula to become and remain mediocre."

+ ***"Following your intuition might not be the sole formula to become extraordinary, but listening to others and conforming each time is definitely the sole formula to become and remain mediocre."***

"There are people who do not seem to be fully impacted by other people's opinions. They hear what everyone around has to say and are objectively able to decide what to accept and what to discard. These are typically people with high self-esteem. This ability to be independent of other peoples' opinions is a key characteristic of a strong mental muscle. As Les Brown said, 'Someone's opinion of you does not have to become your reality'. In fact, some of the people who are working strong on their goals might come across as arrogant. There is a high probability that at their cores, they will be nice people. What you find arrogance might be something they developed over many years as a defense mechanism to keep their vision and goals protected from the world around them."

"As the saying from Andrew Carnegie goes, 'Dealing with people is a lot like digging for gold: When you go digging for an ounce of gold you have to move tons of dirt. But when you go digging, you don't go looking for the dirt, you go looking for the gold.' People will have all kinds of opinions. It is you who needs to stay focused on what kind of responses you are looking for. If you are absolutely certain inside of you that you will succeed and are looking for people who can encourage you, continue to discard all opinions from people who discourage you and keep your eyes firmly set to look for the ones who do not. These are the giants you will stand on the shoulders of. As Isaac Newton said, 'If I have seen further than others, it is by standing upon the shoulders of giants'. Who are your giants, Ron?"

"I have never really given it a serious thought!"

"Ron, it is quite important in life to identify the mentors who genuinely care for your success. Even if you are one of the more positive people and are clued into your heart's voice, you will still have highs and lows, although with lower frequency and intensity than others who have not dedicatedly focused on developing their mental muscles. In times of lows, your giants will pull you out and make you realize that people do not drown by falling in water, they drown by remaining there."

> ***"In times of lows, your giants will pull you out and make you realize that people do not drown by falling in water, they drown by remaining there."***

"Ron, if there was just one skill that if taught to people can make them invincible or unstoppable, it would be this: Getting up each time they fall! Once you decide where you are and where you want to be, it's time for relentless execution. The difference between people who seem to get what they want and the others is that the former group doesn't give up till they get what they want! Their inner sense of strength is so strong and their goals so inspiring to them, that they take every failed attempt as feedback and continue to move on."

> ***"If there was just one skill that if taught to people can make them invincible or unstoppable, it would be this: Getting up each time they fall!"***

Principle 4: Discipline is the key to any worthwhile achievement and a strong mental muscle makes it possible

"Nothing extraordinary can be achieved without disciplined effort. A strong mental muscle is a critical requirement for disciplined action. A soldier doesn't go to war every day, but his daily commitment and effort comes to the forefront when he does."

"Use of mind control to bring disciple in life does not just help make the mental muscle stronger but also leads to an increase in one's overall self-esteem. It is a self-reinforcing loop. The more you show discipline on some task, the more you can progress. The more you progress, the more you add to your self-esteem. The more you add to your self-esteem, the more discipline you show and thus make more progress. There is nothing that erodes self-esteem faster than unfinished tasks. There are so many activities you start to do and then owing to lack of not being able to follow through, you drop these activities midway."

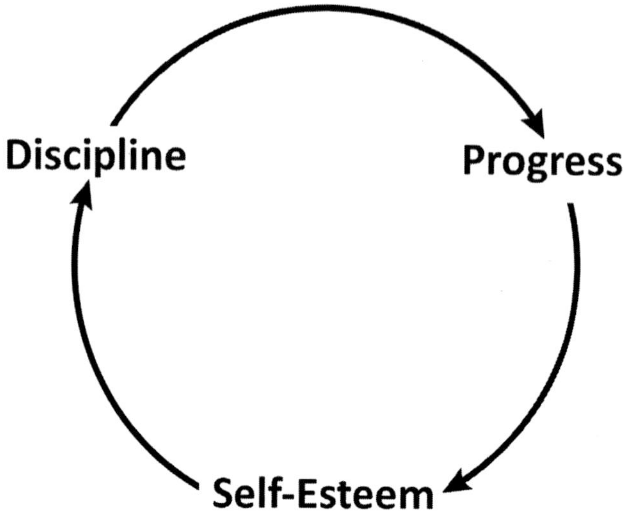

Figure 27: Self-reinforcing loop of discipline, progress and self-esteem

> + *"There is nothing that erodes self-esteem faster than unfinished tasks."*

"Ron, it sounds so simple! But if it really is that simple, 'Why do people not follow it?'"

"Well, most people do not get to kick this off and get left out. As Lao-Tzu said, 'The journey of a thousand miles begins with a single step'. There are really just two things: To get started and to not stop till you get what you want. As Edison said, 'Our greatest weakness lies in giving up. The most certain way to succeed is always to try just one more time'"

"Ron, we covered this earlier. It is same as making better choices. The general understanding that people have for discipline is lack of freedom. Here again, it is an issue with perspective. In the short-term, it might appear as you are making choices that do not look attractive, but in the long-term, you create your future exactly as you want it. How is it a lack of freedom? In fact, it is the ultimate freedom! You are taking the power away from circumstances and getting it in your own hands."

> ***"Discipline might seem like lack of freedom in the short-term; in the long-term, it is the ultimate freedom."***

"Yes, that's true! What do you suggest can be a good way for this?"

"A good way is to start by committing small time durations and waiting for momentum to kick in. If you start by saying that you want to leave coffee for a lifetime now, you will be overwhelmed right at the beginning and will fall flat on day two or three, as you will see a long way ahead. Never frame it as you are going to deny yourself of something, always frame it as having more choices and you are giving yourself something else."

"A better approach is to say you will have something else, say green tea instead of coffee for ten days. Now on day three or four, you know it is just six or seven more days to go making it less overwhelming for you. This will allow you to go past the low point easily and then the positive momentum starts to kick in, so by the time you will be at day ten, you will already start to experience positive impacts of your new habit, that is, having green tea in place of coffee. At this point, you can decide to extend your decision from ten days to thirty days and see how your body continues to respond. At the end of thirty days, you might choose to continue with green tea. Even if you want to have an occasional coffee, you will not feel the same level of addiction and you will have regained your power over your habit. Imagine doing a few activities like this. How much it can boost your mental muscle! Since mind control is such a powerful life skill that once mastered can help you transform your life, we have slightly more exercises today."

"Sure, let's go ahead, I am ready!"

Exercise 1: Conquer your 'meaning assignment mechanism'

"As a creative exercise, I encourage you to do this. Whenever something happens, any significant event in your life, force your mind to create at least four different meanings, two positive and two negative, on what all it could mean. Even within these meanings, adopt meanings along varying degrees. Assign one moderately positive meaning and one highly positive one. Assign one moderately negative meaning and one so negative that it totally paralyzes you into inaction and instant depression."

"Why do you want me to do that?"

"Ron, when you start doing this exercise, you will have two key realizations:

1. You will convince yourself that it is we who assign meanings to whatever happens
2. You will take full control of your mind, totally disempowering it and next time it assigns a negative meaning, you will feel like laughing at it instead of taking it seriously. You will be asking your mind, 'Are you really sure it cannot mean anything else?'"

+ ***"Going forward, as your mind assigns negative meanings, ask it 'Are you really sure it cannot mean anything else?'"***

"Thank you Ron+! This seems to be a powerful exercise. I will ensure that I practise it till it comes naturally to me."

Exercise 2: Constantly keep your 'energizers' handy

"Remember we talked about the days when you just wake up more positive than other days and how you naturally tend to be nice to everyone around? We all have our 'energizers', that is, things that can instantly change our frame of mind and make us feel better. These energizers can be a song that has happy association in your mind or picture(s) of someone you truly love or admire, or something gifted to you by someone, or any other thing that can make you resonate with a higher energy level emotion such as passion, enthusiasm or happiness. A good practice is to make a list of all these items that work for you and keep them handy so that each time you feel low, you can instantly change your state of mind."

"Okay! Let's do this exercise and see what three to four such energizers can be for you."

"Ron thinks hard and comes up with three of them:

1. A song he used to propose to his first girlfriend
2. A book with a handwritten note from one of the girls who he really liked
3. His mother's picture"

"Okay, Ron. I understand the first two. Love is a mighty force that can recognize geniuses within us and inspire us to unleash our giants within. Most people have their energizers as pictures of their spouses and kids which they keep handy all the time in their wallets, phones etc. Your mother's picture is interesting. This is the first time we talk about your parents. What about your mom? You want to talk about it?"

"She is a simple woman in lifestyle yet extraordinary in her expectations from life. She consistently pushed me to be more and did not let me become complacent no matter what I kept achieving."

"That's a great quality, Ron. For most people, their self-images take a massive beating in childhood itself. The influence, we receive from our parents and teachers, plays a key role in how we view ourselves there on."

+ ***"For most people, their self-images take a massive beating in childhood itself."***

"There are two clear extremes within which these people influence us. One is, introducing us to mediocrity and reinforcing it for us or introducing us to genius and inspiring it within us. All parents want the best for their kids and by no means want their kids to be mediocre. However, in addition to this wish, they love their kids so much that their anxiety for them is fairly high. This mix of feelings makes the parents prefer standard options instead of offbeat ones, inadvertently pushing their kids towards becoming 'extraordinarily mediocre' as that path ensures certain amount of guarantee for a comfortable life."

> ***"There are two clear extremes within which these people influence us. One is, introducing us to mediocrity and reinforcing it for us or introducing us to genius and inspiring it within us."***

"Tell me Ron. How would your mom feel about you these days when you are so lost and talk like you already lost the war of life while you have a long way to go?"

"She would not feel good at all."

"So, what makes her feel good?"

"She is genuinely happy when I am fully charged up, bursting with energy to give my best and make a positive difference in everything I do."

"Simple. What can make you to be like that? Do you recall the last time you were like that?"

"Yes, in the final year of my MBA. I had a business plan for which I was in talks with leading venture capitalists in the country. It was the best year of my life. However, for some reason, I decided to take up a job. It was great in the first three to four years but with time, I started feeling that I wanted to do more."

"Okay, Ron. So now on, each time you look at your mother's picture, imagine yourself to be where you were in final year of your MBA, back to the Ron who was charged up and wanted to make a difference. Nothing has changed since. You are the same. The world outside is the same. You have lost touch with the fire within you. In fact, it is not just you. Most people lose this touch with that magnificent source of all possibility inside them somewhere along their way in life. It doesn't mean the source ceases to exist, it just means that we need to re-establish our connection with it. And for you, your mother's picture will do exactly that going forward."

> ***"In fact, it is not just you. Most people lose this touch with that magnificent source of all possibility inside them somewhere along their way in life."***

"Sure Ron+! Now that I relax and try to recall those memories, I can begin to get in touch with the same old Ron after so many years. Thank you for introducing me to this exercise. I will consciously make it a part of my life now and can become the same old Ron whenever I want!"

Exercise 3: Learn positive visualization and mental rehearsal

"A key mental technique that is widely used in sports and business is practising positive visualization and mental rehearsal. Before athletes go into their games, they visualize with full intensity, how the game will unfold, and how they win and how the crowd applauds after they have won. They do this using all their senses, to make it as real an experience as they can. They see the crowd applauding and hear the applauses loud and clear. They imagine what a gold medal would feel like against their chest. As Megan Quann said, 'I have been visualizing myself every night for the past four years standing on the podium having the gold placed around my neck.'

"Some athletes claim that they win their games even before the games start. Essentially, they win in the mind first and then in reality. As Camille Duvall said, 'I train myself mentally with visualization. The morning of a tournament, before I put my feet on the floor, I visualize myself making perfect runs with emphasis on technique, all the way through to what my personal best is in practice... The more you work with this type of visualization, especially when you do it on a day-to-day basis, you'll actually begin to feel your muscles contracting at the appropriate times.'

"The same technique is used in business, especially before meetings and presentations. Some executives rehearse how the meeting is going to be in their minds. They visualize their fellows asking them questions which they are responding to confidently. Doing it over and over in the mind makes the real event go smoothly. Additionally, doing this before the event can help take away some of the anxiety that usually builds up before key events."

+ ***"Doing it over and over in the mind makes the real event go smoothly."***

Exercise 4: Categorize people around you and decide your level of engagement

"You might find this exercise bit disturbing and painful. But trust me it will have a tremendous impact on your life if you do it well. List all the people in your peer group: friends, colleagues, extended family, and acquaintances, that you interact with and categorize them into three groups based on how you feel during and after your interactions with them. Do you feel positive, neutral, or negative? Do they inspire you or drain your energies?"

"Have you heard this anecdote, of the man who wanted to jump down a bridge and commit suicide? Another man saw him, rushed towards him, acknowledged his pain and offered to talk about it if it could make him feel better. They talked for a couple of hours and then both of them jumped off the bridge. You know some people who can have that impact on others. We all do. Avoid these people at all costs! I do not have anything against them. We all have our reasons to be the way we are, but these reasons should not hold us prisoners and keep us tied to negativity, so much so that we spread it to others. I understand that you might like some of these people and might be close to them, which is perfectly fine. Once you are able to take yourself to another level of positivity, you may be able to help them. For now, you will have to detach yourself, undergo your transformation and then help them in theirs. It's like they say on the airplanes: Wear your own oxygen mask before you help others."

"I can appreciate what you are saying here."

"Ron, look at the table that I have prepared. Categorize people and see the actions you need to take. Take your time to prepare the list. You don't have to share it with me if you don't want to."

Table 12: Peer categorization

Category	How do you feel?	Proposed action
A	**Positive / High energy**	Ensure you meet them at regular intervals, whatever is practical given your schedules, say once a week, month, three months etc.
B	**Neutral / Same energy**	Reduce the time you spend with them, if you are spending a lot of time and move it to people in category A
C	**Negative / Low energy**	Decrease the interaction gradually and move time to people in category A as first preference and category B as second preference

Ron prepares the list. He writes the actions he can take to ensure he is able to increase or decrease the association as required. Ron also creates a timeline around them.

Exercise 5: Cultivate your intuition to make it stronger

"This is a very important topic as our intuition connects us to our source. Most people assume that their prayers do not get answered. The truth is that they were never available to listen to the answers! The most effective way to increase your intuition is to start trusting it by listening to and acting on it."

> ***"The single most effective way to increase your intuition is to start trusting it by listening to and acting on it."***

"To be able to listen to it, the first step is to make space for it within our thought train of the 60,000 thoughts that we run in our minds every day. Practicing mindfulness can help increase your faith in intuition. It can be difficult when you begin, so start using the 'switch analogy'. Imagine there is a switchboard in your mind with multiple switches on it for work, family, meditation and the like. When you leave work, visualize in your mind that you turn off the work switch and turn on the family one. When you want to be silent or meditate, turn off all others and turn on the meditate one. Just this one simple technique symbolically instructs our minds to relax. We can thus be fully present wherever we are in the moment. Being fully present is the path to that connection within us."

"On a more tactical level, there are games you can play with your intuition and they are fun as well! Pick some from the list below, or can decide to do all of them on a regular basis:

- ***Who's calling?*** – Whenever someone calls, try to guess in a split second, who it could be before checking it
- ***What's the time?*** – When wanting to check for time on your watch or phone, make a quick guess in your mind, down to the hour and minute and then check it
- ***What's the card?*** – Take a pack of cards and randomly try to predict the next card that you will turn. You can start from the color of the card: red or black, and then with time move on to the suit: Spades, Hearts, Diamonds or Clubs
- ***What's he or she wearing?*** – Guess what people will be wearing before you meet them. Start generic and with time, go to specific details

"You are right! They indeed seem like games! I will start working on them."

With this, the transformational weekend comes to an end. These two days have been quite enlightening for Ron. He got to learn about 'Goals' and 'Mind Control' and really understood himself more on what is really important to him in this life and how he can have the mental strength to pursue it.

Lying in bed with a feeling of newfound clarity, Ron is ready to doze off, and is eager to start a new day. Now he knows what he wants out of it and every day that will follow here on.

10. HOW TO TALK TO YOURSELF? (SELF-TALK, DAY 8)

"If you hear a voice within you saying, 'You are not a painter' then by all means paint and that voice will be silenced" ~Vincent Van Gogh

It is Ron's turn to drive to office. The discussion in the car centers on the getaway that other two guys went to, over the weekend, with their families. They invited Ron as well, but he declined saying that he had family visiting him over the weekend. Now, listening to their discussion, Ron felt like he missed something by not joining them. But, he is quite satisfied with the way he used his time otherwise. The weekend was heavy with a lot of information for him to absorb. He is already starting to see positive changes in him and how he sees the world. He appreciates that though most people in the world believe in circumstances controlling their lives, there can be a few who play an increased role in what shows up in their lives and they create their own circumstances. As Bruce Berton said, "Nothing great has ever been achieved except by those who dared believe something inside them was superior to circumstances."

In the office, Ron watches people closely. For the first time, he sees more causality in all that he sees. He is able to understand why some people produce the kind of results they do in all areas of their lives. He relates their results to their self-image, the beliefs they hold, their charisma, their passion and energy levels, and their mental strength.

Another work day ends. Ron gets back home to his routine of showering, ordering in, dining and getting ready for the discussion with Ron+.

Principle 1: You are not the voice in your head; you are the one who hears it

"Ron, there is a voice in our heads that constantly keeps talking and hardly ever shuts up! What is ironical is that most people do not even realize the presence of this voice."

> ***"There is a voice in our heads that constantly keeps talking and hardly ever shuts up! What is ironical is that most people do not even realize the presence of this voice."***

"Yes, you are right! This is the first time I am hearing someone talk about it!"

"Let's do an exercise right away. Make the voice say, 'Wow, Ron! You are such a super star, I am proud of you!' Now tell me, how does it feel?"

"It feels weird! But yes, I can hear the voice!"

"I am sure you can acknowledge the voice's presence. You feel weird as the voice never really talks to you like that! Now try saying, 'Why do I always screw up?' It's perfectly fine if it sounds familiar. Most people are used to hearing negative things from the voice within."

"Yes, you are right again!"

"A liberating realization is that you are not the voice and can make yourself independent of it. This voice does both. It talks in positive as well as negative tones. Which of the two dominates in your case depends on what you listen to, more. It is like asking, if two dogs fight, which of the two will win? The answer is simple: The one you have been feeding more will win! Research indicates that out of the 60,000 thoughts we have daily, around 80% tend to be negative e.g. 'I am always late', 'My hair can never look good', 'Maybe I should not have said that' and the like. Sounds familiar?"

"Yes of course! Ron+, are you suggesting that we get rid of the negative voice altogether?"

"Most people listen to the negative one more than the positive one. There is nothing wrong with the negative one. It is just a biological mechanism that alerts us when we try to do something new or different or venture out of our comfort zones. The larger objective that voice serves is to do the best for us. Appreciate it for that. What needs to change is when it criticizes us more than necessary and debilitates us from taking action. Each time the negative voice alerts us, we need to listen to it, acknowledge it for expressing its concern and then continue to prepare our plans or act positively. Courage is not absence of fear, it is overcoming of fear."

Principle 2: The words we use to describe it become a part of any experience

"The words you attach to an experience start to define it. Imagine you come from a dinner and you quite liked the food. Try this. Whenever someone asks you how the dinner was, act as if you did not like it and say 'It was terrible'. Do it with four or five people and you will realize that when you think of the dinner yourself, you do not feel good. One of the powerful applications of this observation is to encourage people to assess the vocabulary they use commonly and modify it to make it positive, and test how, with the change in the vocabulary, they are able to change the way they feel about themselves and their lives in general. We will do some exercises around it later today."

> *"The words you attach to an experience start to define it."*

"One of the reasons why our peer group tends to have a huge impact on us is this. We pick up the same vocabulary and talking patterns. Try it for yourself, or maybe you have already observed it. Watch the new words that come into your day-to-day conversations and your thoughts. Check where they came from."

Principle 3: Ask better questions to get better answers

"Successful people ask better questions and hence they get better answers. A lot of people say that they want their relationships to be happy and fulfilling. But the question they repeat in their heads is 'Why is this relationship not working?' or 'Can this relationship ever work?' If you ask these questions, the mind constantly brings the negative aspects into your focus. A better question to ask would be, 'What can I do to make this relationship work?' This will force your mind to seek 'solutions' rather than 'excuses.'"

> + ***"Successful people ask better questions and hence they get better answers."***

"In times of tragedy or loss, people tend to ask, 'Why did this happen to me? Now, you are intelligent enough to realize that this question is not the best one to ask as it cannot elicit resourceful responses. A better question is to ask, 'What is the learning for me in this?' or 'What does this have to teach me?' or 'Now that this has happened, how does it leave me better than I was before this?'"

"The moment we take a higher perspective on life, we understand that there is a larger intelligence in the world and that we will never be able to understand what is going on. Is it not then a good choice to assign positive meanings all the time? Let me rephrase. When you can never know what is going on with full certainty and you are assuming anyway, why not assume something positive that makes you feel better and resourceful to take action rather than something negative that limits your life experience? The more we stay positive, the more we begin to understand how the larger intelligence works. Now, since we are humans at the end of the day, and will never be able to banish all negative thought, we will never fully understand the larger intelligence. Hence, this journey is all about striving, striving to get there as much as we can."

> + ***"When you can never know what is going on with full certainty and you are assuming anyway, why not assume something positive that makes you feel better and resourceful to take action rather than something negative that limits your life experience?"***

Principle 4: It is possible to convert that inner voice into your cheerleader, your coach

"The point I am emphasizing here is this: Your inner voice tends to be critical of you most of the time. Sometimes, to such a high degree that it becomes disturbing. If you can make your inner voice come onto your side, it can go from becoming your worst critic to your best coach. I say worst critic because that's the first level of resistance you face in trying to do anything other than what you do in your little world. On that note, let me build it further. There are typically three levels of resistance that you face when you try to do something unconventional:

- ***Level 1:*** Your own inner voice
- ***Level 2:*** Your circle of close associates i.e. spouse, family, and friends
- ***Level 3:*** The world in general"

"Level 1 is the first one you need to conquer and bring onto your side. If you don't have it on your side, it will be difficult for you to get levels 2 and 3 on your side."

"With changes in your self-image and beliefs, and becoming better at mind control, it is possible for you to train your inner voice to adopt a different style of talking. Instead of critiquing and criticizing, you can train it to talk to you like a coach does."

> ***"With changes in your self-image and beliefs, and becoming better at mind control, it is possible for you to train your inner voice to adopt a different style of talking."***

"Ron+, can you give some examples?"

"Sure. Instead of saying, 'You will never get it right', train the voice to say, 'What do you need to do/ have/ learn to get it right?' Instead of saying, 'People don't care about me or a specific person doesn't care about me', train it to say, 'What can I do to make people care about me or to make that person care about me?' Instead of saying, 'I feel so unhappy', train it to ask questions to help you get to the bottom of why you feel the way you feel: 'How exactly am I feeling?', 'Why am I feeling this way?', 'What can I do to feel differently?', 'How do I want to feel?', 'What can I do to feel that way?' and so on."

"You can train your inner voice to be your cheerleader and to be your coach, helping you clear the mental fog when you feel overwhelmed and to be your best friend who is always with you on this endless journey of growth and contribution."

"Let's work on the exercises around this."

Exercise 1: Self-talk assessment: Listen to the voice

"I want you to start noticing the inner voice inside your head. As a first exercise, I want you to sit in a relaxed place and notice the specifics of that voice in your case. I want you to find out:

- Where do you hear the voice? In your left ear, right ear or in both?
- Whose voice is it? Is it yours, or someone else's?
- What are the patterns that voice uses? Is it always negative, or is it a mix of positives and negatives?
- It is friendly to you or is it harsh on you?
- If it was possible to take that voice outside of you and give it to another person, would you like to have that person next to you all the time or you would have told the person to pack up and go away in just couple of hours?"

"Externalizing the voice, that is, treating it not as a part of yourself but separate from you will already start to initiate a big change in the way you respond to it."

> ***"Externalizing the voice, that is, treating it not as a part of yourself but separate from you will already start to initiate a big change in the way you respond to it."***

As instructed, Ron conducts the exercise and makes a note of the responses for himself.

Exercise 2: Make friends with the inner voice

"Now that you have dissociated from the voice, start to interrupt the habitual patterns in which that voice has been talking. Having done the exercises on self-image, beliefs, passion, goals and especially mind control, you already see the patterns in your self-talk changing. For the remaining part, you are more equipped to interrupt this voice each time it starts to say something that is not aligned with you becoming your best version."

"The positive reinforcement we talked about works wonders in changing human behavior. Each time you are able to convince your inner voice to go from negative to positive, treat yourself to something you like."

> ***"Each time you are able to convince your inner voice to go from negative to positive, treat yourself to something you like."***

"Sure, I will do that, Ron+."

With that, they call off the day. Ron spends some time noticing the voice, and in the process, starts to dissociate from it.

11. HOW TO USE THE GREATEST LEVELER? (TIME MANAGEMENT, DAY 9)

"It's not enough to be busy, so are the ants. The question is, what are we busy about?" ~Henry David Thoreau

This happens to be one of those days when Ron got up happier than he did on other days. He does his morning rituals with the bathroom mirror and shower. He has breakfast and joins the car pool where he starts to share the findings from his reading openly. A friend who started reading too, talks about his experience.

The day in office is normal. Ron is more positive than usual. He finds himself being nicer to everyone and more productive at work in general. Ron gets home, follows his routine, and is ready for the discussion. This is day nine. He realizes that it is just for one more day that Ron+ will be with him. He realizes how far he has come in his quest for self-realization and is keen on making the most of these last two days.

"Ron, today we will talk about time, the greatest leveler. I call it so because no matter who you are, rich, poor, young, old, you always have the same number of hours in your days."

Principle 1: Time management is life management, our use of time either works for us or against, the choice is ours

"The strange thing about time is that if we don't make it work for us, it will naturally work against us. There is a saying 'You don't kill time; it is time that kills you!' Change is a part of life, everything changes. Not all change is for good by default. Progress or positive change needs to be designed. If you lose your money, it is possible to get it back. But, time once lost cannot be regained. If you spend time well today, you can be sure of making money in the future. If you let things be, time can fritter away unless you intervene and make it a point to spend it in a way that you get the most out of life."

> + ***"If you lose your money, it is possible to get it back. But, time once lost, cannot be regained."***

"You will see many people around wasting time as they do not have a vision or clearly defined goals that they want to achieve. If you think you have already wasted a lot of time in the past, and thus there is no point managing it better now, think again! It's like saying, since you didn't have a 10-year vision when you were 30, and now that you are 40, there is no point having a 10-year vision now. Think of yourself at 50! Irrespective of what happened in the past, won't you be better positioned at 50 if you have a vision for the next ten years when you are 40, versus not having it at all? That's the good thing about personal development. Irrespective of what happened in the past, you can always begin afresh. As per the Chinese saying, 'The best time to plant a tree was twenty years ago, the second best time is now!'"

> + ***"That's the good thing about personal development. Irrespective of what happened in the past, you can always begin afresh."***

"Without vision or goals, one cannot understand the spirit of time management. People mistake time management to be an 'add-on' skill that they can have in addition to the core skills they use to earn a living. They think that the objective of learning to manage time better is to be able to squeeze in more things within their days when they really don't feel any need to do it. It is not really that. When one is able to master time, one is able to enhance and enrich the quality of their life. The quality of your life is determined by the quality of your time. When you spend your time on activities that you do not want to do, the quality of your life cannot be too high."

"When you spend your time on activities that you do not want to do, the quality of your life cannot be too high."

"Don't get me wrong and think that I am telling you to become a super-efficient machine that lives life clocked to the minute. I am not. We are humans. We want to laze around sometimes and do nothing or procrastinate at times or just enjoy good things that life has to offer. That's perfectly fine! Remember, even successful people procrastinate, but it is just that they choose different activities to procrastinate on. You will usually find them procrastinating on low-impact activities."

Principle 2: Simplicity plays a key role in managing time better

"Practicing simplicity is a golden rule for time management. Do not get me wrong here. By simplicity, I do not suggest that you should live a simple life and not enjoy the finer things. What I mean is that you should reduce the complexity, as in remove things that prevent you from being mindful and present in the moment. It means to not have your mind flustered with hundreds of things at the same time. You can choose to have fewer experiences in life, so your mind is not cluttered. But, go for the finest experiences that you can manage from a time, money and logistics perspective."

"Remove things that prevent you from being mindful and present in the moment."

"I will tell you about a few considerations that you can have to bring about more simplicity into your life:

- Have less stuff – Most people are in the habit of buying more things than they need. Once you have more things, they will take more of your time. A key approach is to take on a spring clean at home or office once every six months or a year as it may be feasible, to look at everything you have and decide if you use or need it anymore. If you find that you do not need it anymore, do away with it

- Do lesser things – Decide on clear focus areas in your life. Say that you choose three focus areas at this point in your life: job, family and health. It is difficult for people to focus on more than three areas at any point in time. Try restricting them to two or three. Ensure that most of your time is spent making progress on these areas. Within each of these, ensure that you do limited number of activities and do not clutter them a lot. You can then get the maximum impact and fulfilment from all that you are doing
- Streamline your tasks – Get into a habit of grouping related tasks so you can finish them together. For instance, if you plan a trip to the mall, take a few minutes to make a list of all that you need to get done and spend a few more minutes visualizing how you can move inside the mall to do these things, thereby prioritizing them"

"Do you recommend multitasking?"

"Yes, I do but not in the way the term is used normally. I have a subtle distinction to make. A bit of judicious multitasking can save time. But I do not recommend overdoing it as it can start to suck the joy out of doing those things in the first place. As with everything in life, one needs to find their balance, that is, the extent to which they can multitask without losing the point of doing that activity altogether. Try out different degrees of multitasking and stick to the one that works best for you."

Principle 3: Master the art of creating time windows; within each window, be focused and efficient

"Get into the habit of creating time windows. To do that, the first decision you need to take is what would be the smallest unit of time that you would like your life to be organized by. For instance, let it be two hours, one hour, thirty minutes, fifteen minutes or five minutes. We don't want to become machines doing everything efficiently by the minute. We want to experience mindfulness as well. When we do something, we want to experience the joy in that activity rather than just rushing it up to move onto the next. Under this overall guiding principle, choosing one hour as the standard unit works well. This can be a personal choice. Some might like to make it one and a half hours or two hours. There is no right or wrong here."

+ ***"Choosing one hour as the standard unit for time management typically works well."***

"In my view, going under one hour can make you rush everything you do. It can kill the inherent joy in doing anything. I know people who manage their time by fifteen and thirty minutes and they are always stressed. Another reason to not go below one hour is the finding that for anything meaningful to be produced, it typically takes sixty to ninety minutes of focused effort. On the other hand, going up to two hours might lead to a lot of slack time within your activities."

"I understand. Can you give me an illustration?"

"As an illustration, when you plan your day, you can plan it by one hour as your standard unit. Wherever you anticipate more, say forty to forty-five minutes, round it up and take one hour. Though we chunk the day by one hour, I am not saying that you should waste the free time you get in the day. Say you planned for one hour to travel but reached in thirty-five minutes. Now, always have activities that you can build into these bonus time breaks, say reading books on smartphone or tablet. Even if you can manage ten minutes of reading a day and if you learn to speed read, you can finish an average book in five hours. This will imply that you can read one book a month just in your bonus time breaks! That will mean twelve books per year for which you did not even dedicate any time within your schedule!"

"Yes, that will be great! It is like creating additional time!"

"The ability to focus on one task at a time and complete it as is or better than expected remains the biggest determinant of success. If you do not mix work and play, you can enjoy both more as you will be able to experience focus in each activity without being disrupted. When you do one activity at a time, there will be an anticipation or excitement to get to the other activity that continues to provide something to look forward to in your life."

+ ***"The ability to focus on one task at a time and complete it as is or better than expected remains the biggest determinant of success."***

"People these days are more and more distracted. They are not able to put focused effort into a single activity. To me, this is alarming! People spend so much time with their smart devices and make the technology go against them instead of using it in their favor. Smart devices have made it easier for us to see and share how others achieve excellence in their areas of expertise. It hardly adds any excellence to us. On the contrary, it takes away our valuable time that we could have used to create mastery in our own lives."

"Hmm, I appreciate what you are saying. Any views on what can be a good way forward?"

"I am sure that result-oriented people even today are constantly thinking of ways to use technological innovations to help achieve their goals rather than getting distracted and losing focus."

Principle 4: Speed reading can save thousands of hours over a lifetime

"Ron, these days we are bombarded with so much information that it is increasingly difficult to selectively absorb only what we want. In addition, if you are a slow reader, you end up spending a lot of time reading things you should not have been reading in the first place."

"Learning to speed read is a skill that can save you thousands of hours over your lifetime. It enables you to:

1. Quickly scan through something to decide if you want to read it or not
2. Read it quickly for information that you want to get from it"

"Reading is one thing that you cannot escape and you need to do it all the time in both, your personal and professional lives. If you can become faster at it and extract pleasure from it rather than consider it as a pain, you can increase your level of well-being with this one skill by being more resourceful. The first thing that needs to happen to be resourceful is to have a high level of awareness on how things are and how they work."

"Speed reading can enhance your reading speeds up to three times with increased levels of retention. Where a normal person reads at ~200-300 words a minute, with these techniques, it is possible to increase the speed to up to ~600-1000 words a minute with a high level of comprehension."

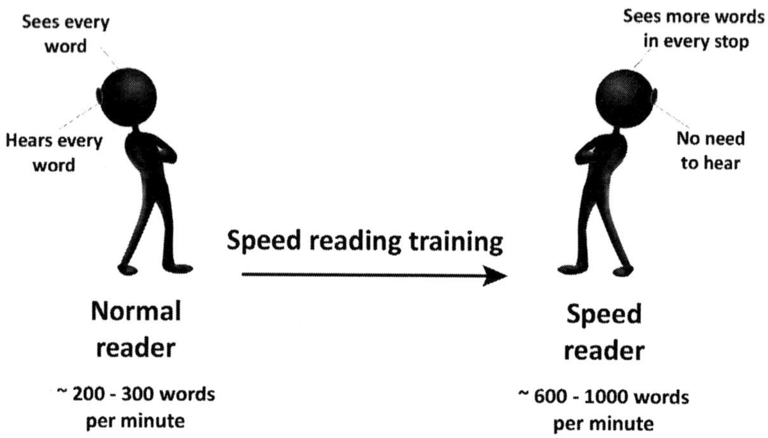

Figure 28: I am a speed reader

"Ron+, can you tell me more about speed reading?"

"Sure! A key principle in speed reading is being aware of your objective behind reading something. Know what you want, and adapt your reading speed in line with it. Once you are clear on your objective, for instance, you are reading for leisure, or for information, or for improving your own language skills etc., you can decide to choose the pace of reading."

> *"Once you are clear on your objective, for instance, you are reading for leisure, or for information, or for improving your own language skills etc., you can decide to choose the pace of reading."*

"Another key principle in speed reading is training your eyes not to stop at every word, but to see more words in every stop to reduce the number of stops you make on a line. This goes hand in hand with breaking the notion that to read something, one needs to hear it in the mind as well. Once you are able to break that, you are set to read a lot more. There are detailed books and software to help you learn this skill. It can make you more productive than you are. Check them out, choose the medium you want to learn it from and incorporate it within your roadmaps."

"Sure, I will do that!"

Principle 5: Worrying is best done in worry or stress windows

"Although this topic has been touched upon in mind control, let's talk about it in the context of time management, as it is one of the key areas where people waste their valuable time. To put it in simple words, 'worrying' is a bad use of one's imagination. Like fear, not all of it is futile. Some level of worry or anxiety is good as it motivates us to be better prepared for the event or activity that is making us anxious. For example, if you have an exam or a meeting in the time to come, it is natural to feel anxious. This anxiety will provide you with the necessary motivation to prepare for it. The answer to the question, 'Is worry or anxiety totally bad for us?' is really not 'Yes'. It depends on the degree to which we experience it. If it propels us into action, then it is good. If it makes us dysfunctional, then it is bad as it paralyzes us and sucks the energy out of us. It really boils down to the ability to keep the overall stress or anxiety to a healthy level and this is where mind control can play a key role."

> ***"Is worry or anxiety totally bad for us? – It depends on the degree to which we experience it. If it propels us into action, then it is good."***

"Let's also understand what are people really worrying about. Look at yourself and people around you. Are people mostly not worrying about things that never happen eventually, or things that got over in the past and not much can be done about them now anyway? I would easily estimate that ~80-90% of an average person's worries are unnecessary and waste valuable time. As Mark Twain said, 'I've had a lot of worries in my life, most of which never happened'"

"A simple strategy to get over the stressing habit is to schedule 'stress or worry windows', that is, windows of time where you will dedicatedly focus on things that are bothering you or stressing you out. Choose a time around late evening to do this, say before dinner. During the day if something starts to bother you, jot it down into a worry book. It is a good strategy to have a dedicated book called the 'worry book'. Once you have your worry book with you all the time, your mind is relaxed that the worry has been captured into the book and that it does not have to continue to process it all the time."

+ ***"During the day if something starts to bother you, jot it down into a 'worry book'"***

"This is a very effective strategy and will lead to two improvements in your life:

1. It will make your days more productive as you know you have a dedicated time to worry, thereby eliminating worry from your other daily activities
2. Doing this dedicatedly, will show you its meaninglessness. Over time, you will naturally skip doing it daily and would only do it on days you are really stressed out with many things clouding your thinking. You will begin to appreciate the wise words, 'Worry is like a rocking chair, it will give you something to do, but it won't get you anywhere.'"

"Yes, I agree!"

"Let's get into the two powerful exercises around time management."

Exercise 1: Time spend assessment: Assess what you can do differently

"Make a list of all that you did with your time in the past 7 days and you can use your preferred unit of time. You can do it by one hour if that is what you choose to use. If you are struggling to capture the items properly, it means that you do not work in time windows but are rather quite unorganized. It is perfectly fine. That's how most untrained people are. Make approximations to complete the exercise. Out of these activities totaling 168 hours in the 7 days, categorize them into the five categories below:

Table 13: Time categories

Group	Category	Description
Group A	**My time**	The time that you spent sleeping, resting and recovering all by yourself, getting ready for the office in the morning. Include the time spent in recreation e.g. watching television, reading your favorite books and the like
Group B	**Family time**	The time that you spent with your family members e.g. spouse, kids, parents
Group C	**Social time**	The time that you spent with your friends, colleagues or other associates in person, on phone or chatting or social networking
Group D	**Work time**	The time that you spent working both at the office and at home as required
Group E	**My time "extra"**	The time that you spent working doing something in addition to your job e.g. taking some courses, enhancing your skillset, personal development time e.g. focusing on health, reading personal development books and the like

"When you do this exercise, against each activity, qualify the time taken into regular or unexpected, that is, the activity is regular, but took longer last week than it does usually. To make it clear, there are some activities that usually take certain amount of time and are expected to take the same amount of time in the future. There could be some exceptions in the previous week due to which that activity took more time, for instance, top management visit to your office for which you had to work more. The idea is to mark out these exceptions clearly."

"There are only these five windows where a person can spend time. You do not have to do it right now as it might take some time to dig out information. You can complete this exercise later. I will tell you what to do once you fill in the table. Once you have it, assess your table and see what it looks like. Let me give you some observations on how this table typically looks like for successful people:

- An average person might not spend any time in category E. Most successful people spend a lot of time here. They understand the value of sharpening their axes rather than getting tired endlessly trying to get the tree down with a blunt axe
- The distinction between category A and E for successful people is quite less. They recreate themselves in activities that add value to them, for instance, if they want to read a book, they prefer reading a personal development book. If they watch television, they prefer watching something that would help them in their work
- Another observation that is not explicit from this table but is true is that these windows for successful people are cleaner than those for average people. Since successful people do not mix work and play, whatever time they classify as work is more likely to be work than an average person who classifies ten hours per weekday as work, where typically ~30-40% is social time, spent socializing with colleagues"

"With these observations in mind, analyze your table to see how you can move time from your other categories to category E. This is where spending time can provide you with a significant advantage and increase your effectiveness and efficiency in all other categories. Additionally, strive towards making your windows cleaner. Try to maximize the opportunity of working while you are at work and spending time with family while you are at home. A lot of stress in peoples' lives comes from having unclean time windows."

> + ***"Strive towards making your time windows cleaner. A lot of stress in peoples' lives comes from having unclean time windows."***

"You do not have to do this exercise every week, just do it once and it will bring awareness into your conscious and subconscious minds about it. You will start feeling an urge to make better use of your time. Now that you have created so many roadmaps in the previous days, you will automatically live with a sense of urgency and make judicious use of your time. You can repeat this exercise in a few months to check if you are on course. If you seriously work on all the roadmaps you have created till now, you will observe three things in your time spend assessment going forward:

- Your time spent in category A will reduce and move to category E
- Your time spent in categories B, C and D might reduce, not because you will reduce your commitment to your family, socializing or work, but because you are cleaner with your windows and are more mindfully present while you are there
- With all the roadmaps, we are building category E items in your life, so your time spent there will increase significantly. It will continue to enhance the quality of your time spent in B, C and D"

"Sure, got it! I will repeat it in a few months."

Exercise 2: Plan in advance: Days, months, and years and follow-up on your progress regularly

"Driven by your long-term and five-year vision, you can create a plan for the first year on what you think is feasible in year 1. This will come from activities you define for yourself to achieve your five-year goal in our discussion around 'Goals'. Do not bother about creating plans for beyond that now. Remember, progress is seldom linear. In fact, this is a mistake that people make when they try to visualize their future selves. They try to extrapolate linearly. Progress comes in step functions, or as I call them, orbits. You cross one to the next one and then onto the next one and so on."

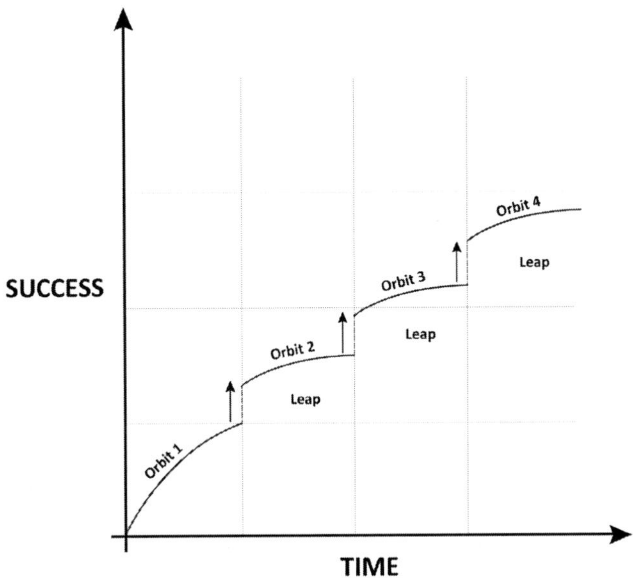

Figure 29: The orbits of success

+ ***"Progress comes in step functions, or as I call them, orbits. You cross one to the next one and then onto the next one and so on."***

"Similar to the magic of writing the goals down, something magical happens when you plan in advance:

- If at the start of the year, you plan key activities that you wish to undertake in this year, you will most likely be able to achieve them in some month or the other
- If at the start of the month, you plan key activities that you wish to undertake in this month, you will most likely be able to achieve them in some week or the other
- If at the start of the week, you plan key activities that you wish to undertake in this week, you will most likely be able to achieve them in some day or the other"

"When you make plans for your day, use time windows as discussed. Create windows of time and strive towards efficiency within them. There is no dearth of planning or organizing or productivity tools in the market. They are available in all formats, from apps on your smart devices to fancy personal organizers available in stationery stores where you can write in with hand if that approach works better for you. Get into the habit of using them."

"Another consideration in planning the day is when to do the most difficult or critical tasks for the day. Though some people might like doing their toughest task of the day first thing in the morning, in my view, you should start with a few easy ones. Once some positive momentum is created in the first few hours, you can move to the toughest task in the day. Another option that is really not recommended is to keep it till later in the day as the anxiety of having to do that task will linger in the mind, tiring you unnecessarily, thereby reducing your energy by the time you get to that activity."

"In terms of when to organize your day, the best practice is to plan the next day's activities the night before. It doesn't take more than ten to fifteen minutes to create a to-do list for the next day and prioritize what you will do when. In addition to feeling more 'in-control' when you wake up in the morning, planning the night before does one more thing. It makes your subconscious mind process information overnight. With that, more often than not, when you start your day, you will have ideas in the morning on how to go about your day that are even better than what you planned. As you continue to work on the plans provided by your subconscious mind and show increased trust in it, you will strengthen its ability to guide you on an ongoing basis."

> ***"As you continue to work on the plans provided by your subconscious mind and show increased trust in it, you will strengthen its ability to guide you on an ongoing basis."***

"Again, you do not have to do this exercise right away for the month and the year. Start with planning tomorrow's day today. I am aware that these discussions with me are taking a lot of your time each day these days. You will have more time after tomorrow when I am gone. You can do the exercises for the month and the year aligning all roadmaps you have created in the previous days with all the activities you want to accomplish and the corresponding timelines."

In line with the principles discussed, Ron starts to work on his plan for the next day, last thing, before calling it a day.

12. DEFINING THE ROADMAP (DAY 10)

With all the discussions over last few days, Ron has gained more perspective in life. His sense of control on things is increasing. He starts feeling more alive as he felt years ago with his wish to become better and contribute back to society, surfacing again.

His time in the office is more productive by the day and he doesn't dislike it as he did two weeks ago. Another day ends and Ron meets Ron+ for their last discussion together.

"Ron, this is our last day together. We have gone through all the essential elements that you require in your transformation and have already started work on bringing them into your daily life in the least disruptive way. Let's now create an overall roadmap to monitor your progress. How about we connect once a month, say start of the month, for an hour to discuss your progress last month and your plans for the current month? We can continue this for twelve months, after which you will be more self-sufficient to run independently with these principles and exercises."

> ***"How about we connect once a month, say start of the month, for an hour to discuss your progress last month and your plans for the current month?"***

"Sure, sounds perfect! I hope I can meet your expectations!"

"Don't meet my expectations, Ron! Raise your expectations, meet them and continue to raise them each time you get there. As I have emphasized already, human beings have a tendency to rise to expectations. When you treat people as average, they will produce average results. When you start to treat the same people as stars, their results improve dramatically. We perform most often to match the expectations of our peer group. Make necessary changes to your peer group to spend more time with individuals that inspire and encourage you. From the experiences of successful people, while they had hundreds of people around telling them they won't make it, they were also able to find a few who told them they will. These are the ones you need to find for yourself. We all need people around to believe in us more than we believe in ourselves. As discussed during our discussion on self-esteem, it is difficult to find people with an abundance mentality, or people who have a belief system where 'life is not a zero-sum game' and 'the pie continues to grow for everyone as more people become successful'. But remember, it is difficult, not impossible."

> ***"From the experiences of successful people, while they had hundreds of people around telling them they won't make it, they were also able to find a few who told them they will."***

"Ron+, by now, I appreciate fully that anything worth having in life does not come easy. These are the same people we identified to be in Category A in your exercises within 'Mind Control'. Once you find them, find a way to be associated with them on a regular basis."

With these words, Ron+ leaves Ron with the two most important things that create positive change:

1. ***The right principles and tools or exercises*** – Ron+ has given Ron the knowledge that he needs on his journey towards becoming Ron+
2. ***The positive kick-start*** – By spending ten days with Ron and ensuring that he does most of the exercises, Ron+ has kick-started the process of momentum building. Once sufficient momentum is built, the probability of people going back to their old habits becomes low

13. A YEAR INTO THE JOURNEY

As agreed upon, Ron and Ron+ had their start-of-month calls to discuss the previous month's progress and current month's plans. As Ron+ had already indicated, the first couple of months were more difficult than the subsequent ones.

It is a year since they first met and it is time for their twelfth and last session. Ron made considerable progress in all areas of his life and is very much on the trajectory to become Ron+ in five years.

Table 14: Ron's progress in twelve months

Life area	Progress
Physical (Health)	Ron is fitter and feels more energetic all the time He has internalized that his body is his means to experience the world and that is why his experience of the world cannot be independent of how he feels within his body He goes for a run first thing in the morning every day of the work week On weekends, he runs and trains even more He practises moderation in his diet, keeping it balanced without taking it to either extreme
Intellectual (Work)	Ron has embraced the philosophy that he works for himself rather than anyone else, so is fully focused on enhancing his skillset and the value he brings to the marketplace Even if his company does not sponsor certain certifications, training programs and event attendances, he chooses to invest in his education and network

Social (Relationships)	As Ron found most of his answers, he has become calm and content within that has made his relationships with his peers stronger He has acquired a new peer group, full of people who are genuinely keen on living life at the highest level. He realizes that it is easier to strive for the best in everything within this peer group He has attracted the woman of his life. He understood that you need to be like the people you want to attract in your life His intimate relationship grows stronger by the day. He understood that one needs to constantly give to make relationships work. They sometimes fight as they both ignore their own preferences and say they want to do things that their partner typically likes, creating situations where neither is ready to give in
Financial (Money)	Ron has understood that his single biggest asset is his ability to add value to the marketplace and earn money for it He has understood that money is a reward for developing expertise in some topic or area and is not something that can be chased directly He has realized that to build wealth, his savings program needs to have two components (i) it should pay him first, that is, before he starts to pay anyone else, this savings amount gets deducted from his income and (ii) it should be automatic, that is, before he sees this money in his account, it should be deducted and invested as per a predefined plan in line with his preferences and life stage

Spiritual (Soul)	Ron regularly takes his spiritual time-outs once a week. This is a time when he shuts out from everything else and sits in silence to reflect if his life is going in the direction he wants to take it in There is some strange sense of fulfilment that humans get when they give back. Within one year, Ron started sharing his learning with others, giving some free coaching and public talks whenever he gets time from his work

"Ron+, I feel sad now that I know you are leaving me!"

"Ron, I am not leaving you! I was always inside you. You just had to bring me out and I am glad you are doing a great job at it. As Michelangelo said, 'Every block of stone has a statue inside it and it is the task of the sculptor to discover it'. Seeing your trajectory, I am sure you will surpass me. That is another insight from the world of self-help and personal development. People usually end up surpassing their vision or goals eventually if they stay committed to their roadmap on getting there."

\+ ***"Ron, I am not leaving you! I was always inside you. You just had to bring me out."***

"Thanks Ron+. It wouldn't have been possible without you showing that strong faith in myself that I can do it. I was lacking that at the time when we first met!"

"It's fine Ron. You are welcome! Now that you have understood these principles and have been able to apply them and transform your life, it is my sincere wish that you share them with others and enable them to become their '+' versions. Hold the torch for others and let them see their own light. Be to others as I have been to you, and you will never lack meaning in your life."

> ***"Hold the torch for others and let them see their own light. Be to others as I have been to you, and you will never lack meaning in your life."***

"You can say that a divine intervention happened in my life and ignited my spark when I realized that I needed to find my answers in the right places. I wish you all the divine strength and hope you will dedicate as much of your time as possible in spreading the message and lighting up more people around you. Formal education can get people a job and money, but it is self-education that can make them wealthy, from all perspectives, physically, intellectually, socially, financially and spiritually."

"As John Donne said, 'No man is an island'. We won't survive in isolation. Each of us has a fire inside and there are ups and downs in everyone's life. Now that you are trained in this, you will get into the lows relatively lesser than other people and would be comparatively more resourceful in pulling yourself out of the lows each time you hit them. But again, you are human! There will be days when you want someone around to pull you up. There are days when even the best trainers in the world tell their peer trainers that they feel lazy and seek their support in training them. That's just our human element and we are all very much Work-In-Progress!"

"It is a natural thing to find your place in the world, and with time, it will become even more difficult. In this age of distraction, everyone around is confused, overwhelmed and more difficult to influence than in the past. The number of options available in everything is exploding and it will become increasingly important for people to be able to find their anchoring in life, otherwise they will continue to increasingly feel lost without even really knowing why. Although this might seem to be the age of quick results, the value of hard work and perseverance cannot be underestimated. The importance of dedicated focus needs to be reinstated into the lives of people. The principles that we discussed will help you do that more effectively. They have been around for hundreds of years and will continue to hold true in the time to come. Remember, future is not built from past; it is built from the present. As Simone Weil said, 'The future is made of the same stuff as the present'"

+ ***"Although this might seem to be the age of quick results, the value of hard work and perseverance cannot be underestimated."***

"Sure Ron+, any final words, something that I should be doing or not so much?"

"Yes, you can stop calling me Ron+. You yourself have become that now!"

They laugh together at how although it sounded really weird, Ron+ insisted on taking that name so that Ron did not feel a sense of dissociation from this enhanced version and is able to relate to it. They agreed on it being a good idea. You too can choose to call your enhanced version as <your name>+ until you manifest that person into reality!

SUMMARY

Pillar	Element	Principles	Exercises
Individuality	**Self-image**	1. Our lives revolve around the concept of our "self-image" 2. An adequate self-image is a requirement for happy and fulfilling life; to individuals with inadequate self-image, the world can be a frightening place 3. We rarely achieve more than we think we are capable of 4. Our self-esteem is like money in our bank accounts; it increases when we make deposits and reduces when we make claims: The key is to constantly make additions	1. Baseline your self-image: Things you like about yourself 2. Design the leap to next level: Things you would like to do 3. Lighten your backpack: Drop the regrets, they tire you out 4. Take the leap to next level 5. Once this iteration becomes natural, start all over again
	Beliefs	1. Our beliefs are the glasses through which we view the world and life (yes, calling them glasses to emphasize that they can be changed too!) 2. Beliefs are self-fulfilling prophecies 3. We can significantly improve the quality of our lives by adopting more empowering beliefs	1. Baseline your beliefs: Make a list of your key beliefs and assess how they have impacted you all these years i.e. categorize them into empowering or limiting beliefs 2. Design the leap to next level: Discard disempowering beliefs and replace them with empowering ones 3. Take the leap to next level 4. Once this iteration becomes natural, start all over again

	Charisma	1. Charisma is the most powerful tool of persuasion and influence 2. Charisma is the sum total of multiple items, all of which can be worked upon 3. Extra-ordinary is a journey, not a destination 4. Having a focus wider than your own self is a key element for charisma	1. Baseline your charisma: Do a current assessment of your charisma level 2. Design the leap to next level: Define the target charisma level 3. Take the leap to next level 4. Once this iteration becomes natural, start all over again
Inspiration	**Passion**	1. It is normal to not have a single passion in one's life 2. An interest becomes a passion not before you fight for it 3. Do not wait for life to give you your passions, bring your own passion to life	1. Baseline your passion: How much passion do you bring to each of your life areas? 2. Design the leap to next level: Think about how much passion you ideally want to bring to each of your life areas 3. Take the leap 4. Potential areas of passion: List the areas you are interested in

	Goals	1. A compelling vision is the first step for all transformation (same as having 'be' goals) 2. It is fine to make 'have' goals as they give a more tangible feel, however, they should never cloud the main 'be' goals 3. Unwritten goals are better known as wishes; goals needs to be written down, specific and time-bound 4. Progress towards your goals daily and have fun on the way	1. Create a long-term vision for yourself, that is, what do you want to 'be' when you are 40 / 50 / 60 along each of the five life areas 2. Work backwards to create a vision for yourself over next five years along each life area 3. Perform a gap assessment between your current and your envisioned self, develop a roadmap with milestones and timelines to bridge it
Intensity	**Mind control**	1. The ability to master our minds and assign empowering meanings is the most important tool in self-help and personal development 2. The power of choice, and we almost always have it, is the second most important tool in self-help and personal development 3. Listening more to your intuition and less to others is critical for mind control 4. Discipline is the key to any worthwhile achievement and a strong mental muscle makes it possible	1. Conquer your 'meaning assignment mechanism' 2. Constantly keep your 'energizers' handy 3. Learn positive visualization and mental rehearsal 4. Categorize people around you and decide your level of engagement 5. Cultivate your intuition to make it stronger

	Self-talk	1. You are not the voice in your head; you are the one who hears it 2. The words we use to describe it become a part of any experience 3. Ask better questions to get better answers 4. It is possible to convert that inner voice into your cheerleader, your coach	1. Self-talk assessment: Listen to the voice 2. Make friends with the inner voice
	Time management	1. Time management is life management, our use of time either works for us or against, the choice is ours 2. Simplicity plays a key role in managing time better 3. Master the art of creating time windows; within each window, be focused and efficient 4. Speed reading can save thousands of hours over a lifetime 5. Worrying is best done in worry or stress windows	1. Time spend assessment: Assess what you can do differently 2. Plan in advance: Days, months, and years and follow-up on your progress regularly

AUTHOR'S REQUEST

I hope you enjoyed reading the book. I would love to hear from you on how the concepts presented herein positively impacted your life. Please feel free to share your thoughts, experiences and insights with me at rosethi84@gmail.com. I will try my best to respond with a personal message.

I thank you again for giving me a chance to talk to you and look forward to maintaining this relationship as we continue to strive towards becoming our best selves.

I look forward to hearing from you. Let's stay in touch!

Best regards,
Rohit